Culture and Morality

CULTURE
and
MORALITY

The Relativity of Values in Anthropology

ELVIN HATCH

COLUMBIA UNIVERSITY PRESS
New York · *1983*

Library of Congress Cataloging in Publication Data

Hatch, Elvin.
Culture and morality.

Bibliography: p.
Includes index.
1. Cultural relativism. 2. Ethnology—
Moral and ethical aspects. 3. Ethnology—
Philosophy. I. Title.
GN345.5.H37 1982 306 82-9624
ISBN 0-231-05588-9
ISBN 0-231-05589-7 (pbk.)

Fred. 25,00/ 22,50/ 6/24/83

Columbia University Press
New York Guildford, Surrey

*Clothbound editions of Columbia University Press books are
Smyth-sewn and printed on permanent and durable acid-free paper.*

for
Deanna

Contents

Acknowledgments

I THANK several people for their help in writing this book. Both Donald E. Brown and Thomas G. Harding have clarified a number of my ideas in conversations about the material, and they have pointed out references that I might have missed otherwise. David Brokensha, Jesús Cardozo, and Elman Service each read drafts of the manuscript and offered comments which fundamentally altered the argument of the work, though perhaps less so than they would have liked. Finally, Sharron Roemer has been indispensable in creating the typescript and giving advice.

CHAPTER ONE

The Facets of Relativism

F R O M the time anthropology emerged in the nineteenth century
as an organized, self-conscious discipline, it has been involved in
a number of controversies of wide public interest. These have had to
do largely with how to conceive the differences among peoples, and
especially how to understand where Western civilization fits in relation to other human societies.

One of the primary issues to engage anthropologists in the last century was race: the best evidence at the time suggested that races differ
in mental ability, and the question was whether or not the dark-skinned
can ever catch up with the light-skinned. Are the lower races forever
doomed to a position of intellectual and moral inferiority, or will they
be able to raise themselves by degrees to the level of high civilization?
For the most part the anthropologists believed they could. A second
major issue was whether these differences among human beings are
God-given or the result of natural causes. Most anthropologists sided
with the uniformitarians in geology and the Darwinians in biology by
arguing naturalistic causation: in their view it was not God's will that
relegated the savages to an inferior status, but the operation of certain
natural laws of human progress that scientific research should reveal.

With the turn of the century the issues changed for a number of
reasons. At first the new controversies were waged primarily among
the anthropologists themselves together with a few other scientists in
related disciplines, and to the outsider the arguments seemed tedious
and esoteric. But by the 1920s, and certainly by the 1930s, the anthropologists were writing and lecturing to a much wider audience.
The issues turned out not to be esoteric at all, and by the late 1930s

anthropology had acquired a reputation among educated people as an intellectually vigorous and progressive discipline. What is more, race was again at the center of controversy. The nineteenth-century theory that races exhibit moral and intellectual differences had been discounted, and differences among people were now explained by anthropologists in terms of cultural conditioning or social milieu. This led the discipline to square off against preferential immigration laws, racial segregation, and U.S. Army intelligence tests, among other things.

Another issue to emerge after the turn of the century had to do with where Western civilization stands in the total gamut of human societies. Not only did the anthropologists now reject that races differ in natural ability; but their evidence led them to question the very criteria by which we distinguish between higher and lower cultures, or between civilized and primitive peoples. Western civilization imagines itself better than other cultures, the argument went, only because it uses its own cultural values as the standard in judging. What we consider progress is not progress at all in the eyes of other people who have been raised with different cultural preferences. So among the educated public anthropologists became associated with a skeptical attitude toward the notion of progress and toward the superiority of Western civilization. They also became associated with another rather controversial principle, that we ought to be completely tolerant of other ways of life. Even what to us appears to be the most exotic or bizarre cultures are as valid and fitting as our own and should be given equal respect. We are not better than they. In short, the anthropologists were offering Western civilization a different self-identity from what had prevailed almost throughout history, and the changes they introduced can reasonably be described as an intellectual revolution.

The anthropologists' proposals about progress and tolerance—and about the place of Western civilization among human societies—are but several closely related facets of the twentieth-century theory of cultural relativism, which is the subject of this book. My purpose is to describe how the theory of cultural relativism or, better, ethical relativism (a distinction I will discuss shortly), came about in anthropology, what it is, how it has been attacked by critics and buffeted by world events, and to suggest a revised version that is acceptable in the closing years of the twentieth century.

Ruth Benedict gave a prototypical account of cultural relativism, and her argument had two parts. First, cultures differ from place to place. In her words, "The diversity of cultures can be endlessly documented." Second, it follows that there are no absolutes, for the principles that we may use for judging behavior or anything else are relative to the culture in which we are raised. To use her words again, "It is a corollary [of the diversity of cultures] that standards, no matter in what aspect of behaviour, range in different cultures from the positive to the negative pole." She gave the act of killing as an example. One might think that people everywhere condemn killing, yet this is not so. If homicide crosses international boundaries, and if diplomatic relations between the two countries have been broken, the killing does not meet disapproval within the killer's society. One may also find customs which prescribe killing the first two children of a husband and wife, or the killing of parents by their children before the mother and father grow old. "It may be that those are killed who steal a fowl, or who cut their upper teeth first, or who are born on a Wednesday" (1934a:45–46).

Melville Herskovits was another proponent of cultural relativism, and his argument was similar to Benedict's (e.g., 1955, reprinted in 1973:14–15). Like her, he began with the point of cultural diversity: in his view it is an indisputable fact turned up by anthropological study that peoples across the world have widely diverse value systems. Therefore, there are no absolute standards or fixed values. "Evaluations are *relative* to the cultural background out of which they arise."

The reason cultural relativism is so crucial is that it challenges the orthodoxies of our civilization. To the confirmed relativist, the ideas of our society (whether moral or existential) are a matter of convention and are not rooted in absolute principles that transcend time and place. Even common sense disappears when the relativist examines it. Common sense is viewed as nothing more than conventional wisdom which varies from culture to culture. It follows that, if someone else's common sense is applied to our way of life, then our practices look as strange and exotic as theirs seem to us.

The way in which cultural relativism challenges our orthodoxies is well illustrated by our attitudes toward speech habits. Middle-class Americans think of their speech patterns as more precise and efficient than those of the less affluent and less educated segments of society. Usages like "I don't got no car" or "He ain't home" are thought to exhibit not only poor form but sloppy thinking as well. Neologisms like "that's cool" and "wiped out" are thought to degrade the English language by confusing the "true" meaning of these words. Yet the linguist would disagree, for he or she would argue that all dialects of our society are fully capable of precise and efficient communication. Our evaluation of these dialects as better or worse is based upon a purely conventional ranking that is more a matter of social class and prestige than of linguistic precision.

Much of the power of the relativist's argument comes from an assumption about the process of enculturation that few today would dispute. Human beings everywhere absorb a conventional perspective from their cultural or social milieu. This perspective includes categories of thought, beliefs, values, and other mental patterns which collectively provide the medium in which we think and perceive. Thought and perception cannot take place without such a conventional perspective, for the intellect requires a tool kit of concepts, theories, standards of judgment, and the like if it is to operate at all. Just as a furniture maker cannot ply his trade without hammers, chisels, and saws, so we cannot use our minds without a body of conventional ideas.

Thought and perception involve two kinds of judgment, and this leads to a distinction between two different forms of relativism. First, a judgment of reality is a judgment about the nature of some piece of the real world—about what it is, not what it ought to be. For example, I may judge that a light bulb is dim, that a person is short, that a glass is broken, or that the Trobriand Islanders have matrilineal clans. A judgment of value on the other hand is an ethical judgment about how something ought to be. As a chaperone at a teen-age party I may decide that the lights are too low and should be turned up. This is a moral question and not a factual one; you will not influence my opinion by investigating the physical properties of the light bulbs at this party, but by arguing with the moral reasons for my decision. In separating the two forms of judgment I do not mean that they are totally independent, for a moral judgment about a matter necessarily hinges on the facts of the case. For example, I may be going blind (or be wearing dark glasses) and think that the lights are dimmer than they really are, and you could persuade me to change my mind by proving that the lights are truly brighter than I thought.

The difference between the two forms of judgment underlies the distinction between the relativity of ethics and the relativity of knowledge. The former is perhaps what first comes to mind when someone uses the term "cultural relativism" without specifying which meaning is intended, and it refers to the notion that the standards that can be applied in judging good and bad or right and worng are relative to the cultural background of the person making the judgment. On the other hand, the relativity of knowledge has it that the existential ideas we have about the world—the categories by which we classify and order it, the theories we have about the way it works, and the like—are conditioned by culture, hence a person's interpretation of events is relative to his or her cultural background.

This book is about ethical relativism and not the relativity of knowledge. Yet the two are so closely related that the latter will continually reappear as the discussion proceeds. Consequently I need to describe it in some detail at the outset. The notion of the relativity of science is a particularly crucial case of the relativity of knowledge and provides a telling example of it. Presumably if knowledge can be absolute anywhere it will be here, since the point of science is to test its ideas against the empirical facts. According to the relativists, however, the distinction between "true" and "untrue" can never be decided in any final sense, for there is no absolute, culture-free standard for deciding which is which. Science rests on a body of a priori assumptions that reflect our own cultural background. For example, it rests on a naturalistic or mechanistic conception of the universe, according to which natural phenomena work by reference to physical principles like gravity, and not by the will of unseen beings. Yet this metaphysical theory is untestable, and there is no culture-free standard to which we can appeal to convince the skeptic from another culture. What is more, scientific theory is a mental construct that represents or stands for certain physical phenomena in the "real" world, and the various parts of scientific theory are articulated according to principles of logic—which are mental principles. It is assumed but unprovable that the physical properties of the world operate according to the logic of our minds (or that they work isomorphically with respect to it).

The relativist would perhaps not deny the virtues of science, for it does work pragmatically. Along with engineering and other specialized branches of knowledge it has made it possible for us to get to the moon and to control at least some diseases; perhaps eventually it will allow the prediction of earthquakes and some control over the weather. On the other hand, the relativist would argue, other theories also work. Theories of witchcraft, for example, are effective in explaining and even predicting events. If a man is plagued by misfortune, he may assume that he has angered a witch who now is causing him harm and that his predicament will continue until he does something about it; consequently he may decide to apologize to the supposed witch for whatever grievance may have provoked the attack in the first place. And matters may indeed improve if he does so. If they do not, of course, it may simply be that he apologized to the wrong witch, or that more than one witch was causing him harm. (Similarly, if an American doctor prescribes a medicine that fails to do the trick, he may try another drug.)

In brief, the fact that a system of ideas works is not proof of its validity. Science may truly be more effective in predicting events than witchcraft, but its predictions may be based on faulty reasoning, and there is no standard to decide what the "right" reasons may be in an ultimate or absolute sense. And just as witchcraft cannot explain all phenomena, neither can science; like the believer in witchcraft, the scientist knows that there are problems which he or she cannot resolve and which we will have to wait to explain.

The no-nonsense realist might respond that the relativist's argument misses an essential point, which is that magical beliefs and notions of witchcraft are more far-fetched than scientific theory. A dispassionate, disinterested third party who is asked to judge—if such a person could be found—would choose science over the other on grounds that it is not as fatuous. Yet it seems hard to imagine that a belief in witches is any more far-fetched than the scientific notions about microorganisms, capillary action, or even gravity. A particularly odd notion to most Americans (certainly as far-fetched as the theory of witchcraft) is Einstein's idea that space is curved.*

Language is another area in which the relativity of knowledge comes into sharp focus. Linguistic relativity (which like scientific relativity is a specific case or sub-set of the relativity of knowledge) is the thesis that the structure of a language orients its speakers to certain features of the world and leads them to ignore others, and to picture reality one way rather than another. Native speakers of two different languages "see" the world and act upon it somewhat differently. According to Benjamin Whorf, for example, Hopi speakers and speakers of European languages have radically different conceptions of time. What is more, he argues, the European language speakers' conception of time is consistent with and has led to record-keeping, time-clocks, calendars, the writing of history, and the like, whereas this is not so for Hopi (Whorf 1956).†

Herskovits remarked that if it is true that "we can never touch the raw stuff of reality," as the philosophers say, then it is "enculturation"—the acquisition of cultural ideas, categories of thought, frames of reference, and the like—"which screens our perception and cognition, [and] becomes our essential guide in the efforts we make to meet reality" (1956, in 1973:84–85).

Whereas the relativity of knowledge pertains to existential ideas, the relativity of values pertains to moral ones. Ethical relativism entails the thesis that "one cannot live a wholly moral life according to one code without being sinful according to another" (Hartung 1954:121); another writer suggests that the essence of ethical relativism is indeter-

---

* For an enlightening discussion of some of the issues involved in contrasting science and witchcraft, see Jarvie 1970 and Winch 1964.

† For a summary of some of the recent research on linguistic relativity, see Cole and Scribner 1974.

minacy: within the sphere of morals, there are no definite answers
(Edel 1955:30). Herskovits (1958, in 1973:56) wrote that cultural relativism developed because of

> the problem of finding valid cross-cultural norms. In every case where
> criteria to evaluate the ways of different peoples have been proposed, in
> no matter what aspect of culture, the question has at once posed itself:
> "Whose standards?" . . . [T]he need for a cultural relativistic point of
> view has become apparent because of the realization that there is no way
> to play this game of making judgments across cultures except with loaded
> dice.

Ethical relativism is generally conceived as standing at the opposite
pole from absolutism, which is the position that there is a set of moral
principles that are universally valid as standards of judgment. One
absolutist ethical theory is the traditional Christian view that right and
wrong are God-given, and that all people may be judged according to
Christian values. A wide range of purely secular ethical theories have
also developed. For instance, the utilitarian theory bases ethical judgments on the principle of doing the greatest good for the largest number of people; a law is judged good if it benefits the majority of society
and not just a small portion of it. Another school of thought builds
on the notion of self-actualization: human actions can be judged good
or bad on the basis of whether they contribute to the individual's personal development.

Moral systems consist of beliefs and convictions about what is right
and good in an ultimate as opposed to a technical, practical, or instrumental sense. For instance, if I go into a store and a clerk is especially
helpful in showing me where to find what I want, I will judge his
actions as good on instrumental grounds. He is useful to me. The
store owner will also evaluate his actions as good on instrumental
grounds, for by satisfying a customer the clerk is helping the store to
make money. It may also be that the clerk will go beyond sheer business considerations and show a genuine concern for my personal welfare—say, if he refuses to sell me what I ask for because he thinks I
will use it in a way that is unsafe. His action now can be judged on
strictly moral grounds, for his concern for me is good in itself and is

not a means to an end. Similarly, I may judge the work of a furniture maker to be very good in that the pieces he makes are crafted so as to stand up well under heavy use. I am judging his labor on purely technical grounds. On the other hand, I may make moral judgments about his work. I may consider good craftsmanship as commendable in itself, and I may hold him and his labor in high esteem as a result. The furniture maker may even choose to make less money from his work than he could if he lowered his technical standards, and I might make the moral judgment that this is good.

It is the *content* of moral principles, not their existence, that is variable among human beings. It seems that all societies have some form of moral system, for people everywhere evaluate the actions of kinsmen, neighbors, and acquaintances as virtuous, estimable, praiseworthy, and honorable, or as unworthy, shameful, and despicable. These evaluations take objective form as sanctions, such as open praise or rebuke; and in extreme cases, violence and execution. The ubiquity of the moral evaluation of behavior apparently is a feature which sets humanity apart from other organisms. It would be difficult to imagine squirrels, say, or lizards, exhibiting moral judgments of the kind that seem to be universal among human beings. Presumably non-humans evaluate one another only as threatening, useful, and the like.

The term "relativity" is often given a third meaning, that of historical relativism. In anthropology the label of "relativist" is sometimes applied to a person who has the view that each culture is unique, that there are no regularities or generalizations that can be derived from the comparative study of cultures, and that anthropology therefore is not a generalizing science. The institutions of each culture are thought to be relative to the historical background of that culture. The critics of this view argue that, if true, it means that anthropology can never be a theoretical discipline and will always be limited to purely descriptive studies; anthropologists may fill the libraries with rich accounts of exotic practices, but their researches will have no scientific relevance beyond the culture that is described and can never contribute to a greater understanding of mankind in general. These critics go on to argue that historical relativism rests on the mistaken assumption that simply because two phenomena are different they cannot be compared. No two phenomena are ever perfectly identical—whether they be pencils, jet aircraft, frogs, or lineage systems. But by the process of selection and abstraction it is possible to rise above the uniqueness of cultures and attend to those features that they have in common. The key is to isolate conceptually what is significant for analysis and not to be overwhelmed by differences in detail. Just as the dissection of several frogs should enable us to generalize about frogs as a whole, the careful comparison of several lineage systems should lead to generalizations about institutions of that kind (Kaplan and Manners 1972:5–8).

At first glance it might seem that historical relativism is quite separate from the other two, since what is at issue here is simply an empirical question of whether or not regularities will emerge from the comparative study of societies. Is it true that we can contribute to a general theory of kinship by comparing the kinship systems of the Trobriand Islanders and the Iroquois Indians? Or are these two systems in fact as different as snow flakes (or as images in a kaleidoscope)? On the other hand, the question of historical relativism can also be seen as a sub-set of the relativity of knowledge. Behind the historical relativist's argument for the uniqueness of cultures is the point that the search for scientific generalizations in anthropology requires valid comparative categories—categories of thought which transcend a given tradition and which apply to cultures in general. Yet the categories we have (such as the concept of kinship system) are rooted in our culture and may be quite inappropriate when applied elsewhere. In other words, to the relativist, the very conceptual tools we must use to conduct comparative research are culture-bound and are not valid in studying other peoples.

Historical relativism means that our understanding of human behavior and of social affairs generally is relative to our cultural perspective. Even our interpretation of ourselves is relative—our view of our own institutions, and of our own history, will change as time passes and as our patterns of thought change. In the area of human affairs, no objective, detached observation is possible. This is true not only for the vacationer or businessman traveling abroad, but for the anthropologist, historian, and journalist as well. It follows that when it comes to understanding mankind, our civilization cannot lay claim to superior forms of knowledge.

Ethical relativism, the relativity of knowledge, and historical relativism are the three main varieties of cultural relativism, and the literature on this general subject can be very confusing since the cover term—cultural relativism—is often used to refer to any one of them, and it is not always clear which. To make matters worse, there are still other extensions of the term. One sometimes reads of relativists in the study of kinship systems and personality structure, for example, which refer to anthropologists who hold that kinship and personality types differ for each culture due to the vicissitudes of history. By and large these other usages of the term are like scientific relativity and linguistic relativity in that they can be viewed as sub-sets of one of the three main varieties of cultural relativism.

Methodological relativism is yet another use of the term, and it stands quite apart from the others. This is not a theoretical issue concerning the nature of values, knowledge, or culture, but has to do with procedures of research: methodological relativism is the thesis that one should try to shed one's own cultural point of view in visiting another culture in order to avoid misunderstanding what is being studied—one's own perspective may get in the way of accuracy and should be held in abeyance until the research is finished. Note that a person may comfortably adhere to the principle of methodological relativism while rejecting the relativity of values and knowledge. For example, a person could hold that another people's conception of the world is completely inadequate, but still adhere to methodological relativism by not allowing this conviction to cloud his findings. Methodological relativism is not unique to anthropology, of course, for it applies equally to such fields as physiology and medicine. A cancer specialist is surely opposed to the disease he studies but does not allow this to influence either what he observes in the laboratory or concludes in the analysis.

This book follows a course that moves back and forth between the historical and philosophical points of view. Chapter 2 begins as a historical account of the nineteenth-century context out of which cultural relativism emerged. I re-create several main elements of late nineteenth-century thought, such as the way human beings in general and Western society in particular were conceived, and then I show how these ideas were modified toward the end of the century as a result of some basic alterations in the social, economic, and political milieu of Europe and the United States. I next describe how cultural relativism emerged in American anthropology as part of these turn-of-the-century developments—it was to an extent a revolt against nineteenth-century certainties; how the theory of relativity was conceived by the American anthropologists, and how it was argued; and how human beings and human behavior were conceived now that the nineteenth-century ideas were rejected. I then turn to the philosophical mode to consider the logical structure of the relativity of values taken as a moral theory; by and large, it seems, philosophers see little virtue in it, and I show why. Still in the philosophical mode, I now pose the major dilemma of ethical relativism, which is that it leads us to approve such behavior in other societies as violence and torture, which is clearly not what the theory was intended to do, and I suggest a way out of this dilemma. Next I move back to the historical mode, tracing what has happened to ethical relativism since about the beginning of World War II, for it seems that as an ethical theory it has been criticized and modified almost beyond recognition; I try to show how this happened by describing the larger context of national and world events outside the discipline. Finally, in the last chapter, I set out what I think is a reasonable point of view to fill the partial void left by ethical relativism, which by the 1980s seems more often to be repudiated than upheld. In this last chapter I ask where we may stand today on the critical issues of human values, tolerance, and progress.

CHAPTER TWO

The Historical Context

CULTURAL relativism did not appear suddenly out of a void, nor was its appearance fortuitous. It has its roots rather in certain developments that were underway at the beginning of this century, and it can be understood better by looking into the processes behind it. In re-creating this historical background I focus chiefly on Britain during about the last half of the last century, because the issues that cultural relativism was a response to were very clearly developed in British intellectual life at that time.

England of course held a prominent position in nineteenth-century world affairs. Crane Brinton writes that the nineteenth century "is the great century of English power and prestige. The Englishman set the tone even for those 'lesser breeds' who hated him. The ordinary Englishman of the middle classes is the most successful, most hopeful, in many ways most representative of *Homo sapiens* in the last century" (1950:427). Britain controlled the seas, and this was an age when overseas colonies and commerce were crucial; the Western world experienced a degree of stability and peace during much of this time largely because Britain's preeminence was unchallenged. Britain in the nineteenth century was also at the center of the worldwide process of industrialization; nowhere else was industrialization as advanced or its effects as prominent.

And Britain was a center for intellectual and scientific developments—perhaps not *the* center, which would have to be Germany (Hughes 1958:42–51), but important nevertheless. For example, geology had become a leading discipline during the first half of the century, and by mid-century British geologists including Sir Charles Lyell had thoroughly transformed European conceptions about the nature of the earth and its history. They rejected the biblical history of the earth, substituting a variety of perfectly natural (and very gradual) processes like erosion and slight earth movements for the catastrophic events reported in the Bible, including the Great Flood. Later in the century biology received the spotlight, especially as a result of the profound changes brought by one of Britain's best-known scientists, Charles Darwin—changes not only in biology but in the Western view of the world and of man's relationship with nature. Darwin's thesis carried the implication that living organisms were not created by God in a single stroke at the same time that He created the earth, but that they gradually evolved by the play of natural forces, or natural selection. Biology shared the spotlight with the growing discipline of anthropology in Victorian British intellectual life. Anthropology helped reshape the European world view in a way similar to geology and biology. An electricity filled the air when anthropology was discussed, and this was because of its message—a very explicit one—that human affairs are explained not by reference to the will of God, but by the perfectly natural process of cultural evolution.

Several themes permeated Victorian British thought and are important for understanding the development of cultural relativism. These were assumptions, or "givens," which apparently were considered too obvious to need defense or analysis. The first is the notion that the universe is meaningful. It was assumed that a design or plan of some kind can be found behind reality, so that events are neither fortuitous nor purposeless, but express some overall principle and thus make very good sense. To a degree this was but an extension of an old principle of Christian thought, which is that the world—and the universe as a whole—is the setting for a magnificent drama that God has designed. All creatures on earth, from the lowliest insects to human beings, were created by God as part of an overall plan. Even such "natural" events as severe winters or droughts, or destructive epidemics, are part of this plan, for these are inflicted upon the world in response to human misdeeds.

During the Victorian era God was removed from the magnificent drama of the universe, and phenomena of all kinds were now con-

ceived naturalistically. Or at least this was true for the leading intellectuals like Darwin and Huxley who, of course, were engaged in
heated debate with their religious counterparts. If God played a role
at all it was to set natural processes like gravity in motion, whereupon
He retired from events and left us to discover their order by ourselves.
Yet it was still assumed that it all did make sense somehow, that there
is a plot behind the ensemble of nature. The world is something more
than a series of purposeless accidents.

Darwin's theory of natural selection is illustrative. Darwin's thesis
was that the individual members of a species which are more highly
adapted will produce a larger number of viable offspring than the others. Their physical, heritable features will therefore be more promi-
nently represented in succeeding generations, and thus the species will
gradually evolve in the direction of progressive adaptation. This theory
contains a very clear plot. Such biological features as body size and
coloration are not random or pointless, like the peculiarities of the
two-headed man or the fat lady in the sideshow. They have survival
value. The lizard, giraffe, and sea otter are not mere oddities. Even
if God cannot take credit for earth's creatures, there is still a fundamental meaningfulness to all that exists.

Perhaps an even better illustration of the assumed meaningfulness
of natural phenomena appears in the work of Herbert Spencer, who
combined philosophy, natural science, psychology, sociology, and anthropology into a single framework. This he called the "synthetic philosophy" because it was supposed to synthesize all knowledge according to a unitary principle. The principle was evolution (see Carneiro
1968). According to Spencer, evolution is a process of change from
simple to complex, from homogeneity to heterogeneity. He wrote:

> Whether it be in the development of the Earth, in the development of
> Life upon its surface, in the development of Society, of Government, of
> Manufactures, of Commerce, of Language, Literature, Science, Art, this
> same evolution of the simple into the complex, through successive dif-
> ferentiations, holds throughout. From the earliest traceable cosmical
> changes down to the latest results of civilization, we shall find that the
> transformation of the homogeneous into the heterogeneous, is that in
> which progress essentially consists. (1857:10)

The solar system is an example (pp. 10–11). Spencer writes that the matter out of which sun and planets are composed was originally diffused more or less evenly (or homogeneously) through space, and only gradually did it become concentrated as a result of gravitational attraction. Yet the atoms did aggregate, very slowly, until finally there existed the system of sun, planets, and moons. The present solar system exhibits far more heterogeneity than existed at the beginning, for the celestial bodies differ in size, distance from the sun, velocity, and temperature. Spencer wrote: "We see what a high degree of heterogeneity the solar system exhibits, when compared with the almost complete homogeneity of the nebulous mass out of which it is supposed to have originated" (p. 11).

Another place where Spencer found the process of evolutionary diversification was in the history of the earth (pp. 11–14). Originally a molten mass, relatively homogeneous in composition and temperature, it slowly cooled, with the result that a thin, temperate crust formed on the surface. Condensation of moisture at the two poles was another source of differentiation, as was the progressive deposition of sedimentary strata. These strata in turn have been upended and distorted by the movements of the earth's crust. Mountain chains appeared and grew, and so on. Plants and animals have gone through a similar process, for the earliest living forms were quite simple (pp. 14–17). The "latest and most heterogeneous creature" to appear out of this process was man himself. What is more, mankind has become more heterogeneous through time by the multiplication of races and by their progressive differentiation from one another (pp. 17–19). Civilization exhibits the process of evolutionary diversification (pp. 19 ff.). In the lowest tribes we find "a homogeneous aggregation of individuals having like powers and like functions. . . . Every man is warrior, hunter, fisherman, tool-maker, builder; every woman performs the same drudgeries" as other women. But soon differentiation appeared, inasmuch as chieftainship and authority developed. Certain persons and groups also became specialized in economic pursuits, which brought about what we now call the division of labor.

Spencer believed he had isolated the one principle that unified all knowledge and that lay behind all phenomena—from the heavenly bodies to modern capitalism. Here was the great plan behind all things.

Yet what is the point of the grand process of differentiation? In Spencer's mind was there a deeper significance to it—or was the pattern of growing complexity and heterogeneity merely a fortuitous datum that could be analyzed no farther? I think not. For instance, take the development of the earth's form. Not only was the earth initially undifferentiated, it was utterly uninhabitable. Yet now we find fertile river valleys, rich mineral deposits, Alpine meadows, and seaside hideaways. Surely the present condition was preferable to Spencer, if only because it facilitated the appearance and proliferation of the most intelligent and advanced creature on earth, *Homo sapiens*. The evolution of civilization also was far from a neutral fact to Spencer. In his view the higher societies are more intelligent and more productive; their members enjoy greater material comfort and all-round happiness. Here, then, was a very general (and glorious) characteristic of the process of evolutionary diversification. This process brings about increasingly superior forms, superior in the sense that *Homo sapiens* is preferable to chimpanzees and gorillas, that civilization is preferable to savagery, and that modern London (or even Manchester) is preferable to the original surface of the earth.

A second theme permeating Victorian British thought was closely related to the first. This was a very strong sense of human self-importance, or a belief that mankind is a very special creature in the overall scheme of things. Like the first, this goes far back in Christian thought, although it reached its peak in the nineteenth-century British milieu. The historian Arthur O. Lovejoy describes this theme as it appeared somewhat earlier, especially in the eighteenth century (1936:186–88). He refers to it as an anthropocentric teleology, meaning the belief that all things were created for man's benefit. To illustrate, Lovejoy quotes from a late seventeenth-century Protestant theological work:

> If we consider closely what constitutes the excellence of the fairest parts of the Universe, we shall find that they have value only in their relation to us, only in so far as our soul attaches value to them; that the esteem of men is what constitutes the chief dignity of rocks and metals, that man's use and pleasure gives their value to plants, trees, fruits.

Lovejoy cites the case of the French theologian Fénelon, who wrote that both plants and animals were made specifically for the use of man. Take, for example, the wilder beasts. These serve partly to cultivate physical skills and courage in the people who hunt them. But they also serve as an outlet for man's fighting propensities, and thus as a means for preserving peace: nature has provided fighting creatures for us to kill in order to relieve us from killing one another.

James Hutton, the eighteenth-century Scottish geologist who preceded Lyell in questioning the traditional Christian views about the earth's history, believed that the processes of geology should be seen in relation to human interests. For example, Hutton argued that erosion serves to wear away the very continents that God has created, and that there is good reason for this. Erosion serves to bring about the dissolution of rocks, which is necessary for the formation of soils, which in turn is needed for the growth of plants. Plants, now, provide animals with food. And both plants and animals are beneficial to mankind (Greene 1961:86–87).

Louis Agassiz, a zoologist and one of the leading scientists in the United States in the nineteenth century, serves as another illustration. He argued that the animal kingdom developed according to a deliberate plan of the Creator, in that He created animal forms in a succession of stages from the most rudimentary to the highest, which of course is mankind. All the stages had a purpose, in that they were but steps toward our creation. So when the most primitive forms of life began on earth, the appearance of human beings was to be the final goal. Agassiz wrote:

> Coming to the noble form of man we find the brain so organized that the anterior portion covers and protects all the rest so completely that nothing is seen outside, and the brain stands vertically poised on the summit of the backbone. Beyond this there is no further progress, showing that man has reached the highest development of the plan upon which his structure was laid. (1866:108–9)

The Victorian tendency to glorify man was particularly manifest in the widely held opinion that what sets us apart from other creatures is our mastery over nature, which in turn is due to our intelligence. Unlike other organisms we have the brains to subdue nature (for example, we can put on clothes in cold weather and thus survive quite comfortably in environments for which we are not naturally suited), but also to turn nature to our own use. For instance, we can extract ore from the earth to make metal tools, and we can raise cotton to manufacture clothing.

This was the age of the machine, and mechanical devices and mechanical power gave force to the belief in the importance of mankind. A signal event of Victorian England was the Great Exhibition in 1851, held at the fabulous Crystal Palace in London's Hyde Park. The Exhibition took as its theme the technological achievements of the day and had an enormous public impact. It is even possible to suggest that the development of machine production helped stimulate the sense of human power, for the machine truly did give control over nature (Russell 1945:728). Today we know that this control has its limits—but it was not so evident to the Victorians.

A third theme permeating Victorian thought is closely linked to the other two. This was a very strong tendency to glorify Western, modern, industrial society—to single us out as unique among the peoples of the world. By the 1860s this idea about our own superiority was elaborated in a full-blown theory of anthropology, the nineteenth-century cultural evolutionary theory mentioned earlier, which took the notion of social hierarchy as a main feature. The various peoples around the world were not simply different from one another (and from us), it was thought, but the differences among us are of a hierarchical order. Human diversity runs from very low savagery to high civilization, and generally three separate stages were singled out. Savagery was defined as the stage of hunting, barbarism began with the domestication of animals and crops, and civilization appeared with the advent of writing.

This notion of social hierarchy was the reformulation of a very old pattern of Western European thought, the idea of the Great Chain of Being, according to which the universe is made up of a continuous series of forms—from the very lowliest ("which barely escape nonexistence") to "the highest possible kind of creature" (Lovejoy 1936:59). In its medieval form the Great Chain of Being was directly associated with God, for it was believed that He created the world in full abundance, which meant that He left nothing uncreated, no gaps in the chain; creation achieved perfection in that the entire range of conceivable diversity was brought into being. Nineteenth-century cultural evolutionism entails roughly the same idea, but it is secularized. Human societies exhibit the full range of possible types, from lowest savagery to high civilization, and the sequence is governed by scientific laws of evolutionary development.

This leads to another feature of nineteenth-century cultural evolutionary theory, the notion of progress. Again, this did not originate in the nineteenth century, for it had appeared at various times in Western history, especially during the eighteenth-century Enlightenment. In Enlightenment thought it was believed that the course of human history was one of continuous advancement, that this had been achieved by great effort, and that this progress was still going on and would continue by active social engineering. Some of the greatest minds of that age (including Voltaire, Montesquieu, Rousseau, and Adam Smith) set out to improve civilization by formulating new and sometimes radical schemes of education, politics, and economics.

The idea of progress lost much of its force as the French Revolution and its subsequent turmoil left Europe stunned and demoralized. In roughly the first half of the nineteenth century very little was written about a pattern of improvement in human history, for what predominated now was the older Christian view of degenerationism, according to which human history was a matter of decline once Adam and Eve were cast from the Garden of Eden. The biblical view was that the differences among human populations represent the degrees to which different peoples had fallen—the most savage peoples were the most degenerate, the most civilized were the least. Yet by mid-nineteenth-century this idea came under attack and was eventually replaced by the cultural evolutionary theory that was being formulated by the new discipline of anthropology. A primary thrust of the new discipline was to establish that it is progress, not degeneration, that accounts for the different forms of culture around the world.

A last feature of the nineteenth-century anthropological theory of cultural evolution was the notion of racial intelligence. Let me shift once more to the eighteenth-century Enlightenment to elaborate. The Enlightenment thinkers were not much different from the later Victorians in viewing Western society as an advancement over, say, the savagery of Africa or of the New World. The North American Indian, for example, was thought to enjoy fewer comforts and less security, and to have a less happy and fulfilling existence generally, than the educated Parisian. The Enlightenment *philosophes* also believed (like the Victorians) that what had given the Europeans their elevated position was the power of thought (the *philosophes* would have used the term "reason"). What is more, they assumed that reason "is the same in all men and equally possessed by all" (Lovejoy 1936:288), in that all men everywhere have the same capacity to recognize the virtues of civilized life over savagery and to improve their condition accordingly. But if that is so, why did savagery persist in some places? Perhaps there was no standard answer among eighteenth-century writers, but a common view was that the environment is the primary cause. If the savage child were removed from the wilds of his native homeland and raised in the more stimulating environment of Paris, he (or she) would be quite as refined and reasonable, and would show just as good judgment, as his peers in the country that adopted him.

By the middle of the nineteenth century, race was inserted into this formula (Stocking 1971). The savages had not improved themselves as much as civilized people because the savages did not have the intelligence to do so. The savage child raised among the educated in London (for now the center of world affairs had shifted from Paris) simply could not keep up.

Who were these savages? They were dark-skinned peoples—Australian aborigines, New Guineans, Maori, Black Africans, American Indians, and so on. The more civilized and intelligent human beings were light-skinned. The clear implication was that dark-skinned people living in countries like the United States were inferior to their light-skinned neighbors on the other side of town.

Environment was not entirely eliminated from Victorian thinking about mental differences among peoples. The view of Edward B. Tylor (1881:113) is representative of one important strain of Victorian thought. According to Tylor, the dark-skinned savages are indeed racially inferior, but this itself has an environmental cause. He set up the following possibility: at the earliest beginnings of human forms "there were regions whose warmth and luxuriant vegetation would have favoured man's life with least need of civilized arts." These were notably benign locales, and as such did not challenge the intellect for survival. The "civilized arts" were not needed. But then, he continues, populations began to spread to cooler—and more demanding—climates. He concludes, "It may perhaps be reasonable to imagine as latest-formed the white race of the temperate region, least able to bear extreme heat or live without appliances of culture, but gifted with power of knowing and ruling which give them sway over the world." Whereas the earlier Enlightenment view assumed that the new-born black infant was fully capable of civilization if given the right upbringing, Tylor's view was that it would be some generations before racial differences in intelligence could be overcome—a process that would be accomplished, in his view, according to Lamarckian principles of inheritance. Some of Tylor's critics had a far less benign view of racial diversity. To them these differences in moral and intellectual ability are ineradicable; the less civilized peoples will never be improved and should be content with a life of legal and political subservience to their light-skinned superiors (Stocking 1968a:115–17; 1971).

Herbert Spencer's views about human diversity resembled Tylor's and illustrate late nineteenth-century thinking with respect to racial intelligence. In one particularly revealing passage, Spencer (1897 1:79–82) compared intellectual life with (of all things) eating. He suggested that the higher creatures are very selective in their choice of food, taking only what is nutritious for them. On the other hand, the lower organisms consume great quantities of matter in indiscriminate fashion on the principle that if they ingest a sufficient volume, eventually enough of what is good for them will find its way into their stomachs. Human beings are the most selective organisms, and the highly civilized peoples are even more selective than the lower ones. The highly civilized person is so discriminating that he will separate the inferior portions of food on his plate and leave them uneaten. Similarly, the higher animals exhibit greater selectivity in observing and "ingesting" facts; they are more able than lower organisms to discriminate between the significant and insignificant and to arrive at valid conclusions from the facts. Spencer wrote:

The psychically higher, like the physically higher, have greater powers of selecting materials for assimilation. Just as by appearance, texture, and odour, the superior animal is guided in choosing food, and swallows only things which contain much organizable matter; so the superior mind, aided by what we may figuratively call intellectual scent, passes by multitudes of unorganizable facts, but quickly detects facts full of significance, and takes them in as materials out of which cardinal truths may be elaborated. (p. 80)

Spencer illustrated this by comparing the very intelligent with the less intelligent and presumably less affluent in his own society. Since lesser minds are not as capable of absorbing genuinely significant facts, they have no appetite for them. They have no taste, say, for the experiments of the physicist, which they find too concentrated and hence indigestible. On the other hand,

they swallow with greediness the trivial details of table-talk, the personalities of fashionable life, the garbage of the police and divorce courts; while their reading, in addition to trashy novels, includes memoirs of mediocrities, volumes of gossiping correspondence, with an occasional history, from which they carry away a few facts about battles and the doings of conspicuous men. By such minds, this kind of intellectual provender is alone available; and to feed them on a higher kind would be as impracticable as to feed a cow meat. (p. 81)

If we descend even farther down the scale of human intelligence we come to primitive peoples:

A still greater attention to meaningless details, and a still smaller ability to select facts from which conclusions may be drawn, characterize the savage. Multitudes of simple observations are incessantly made by him; but such few as have significance, lost in the mass of insignificant ones, pass through his mind without leaving behind any data for thoughts, worthy to be so called. (p. 81)

Savages observe well enough, but they cannot deduce much from what they see. Spencer quotes Mr. Galton who described the intellectual ability of one primitive person he had observed. This person "knew the road perfectly from A to B and again from B to C [but] would have no idea of a straight cut from A to C: he has no map of the country in his mind, but an infinity of local details" (p. 82).

Very closely tied to nineteenth-century cultural evolutionism—and another indicator of the belief in the superiority of the industrialized countries that pervaded Victorian thinking—was the concept of culture. The term was first defined by Tylor in 1871 as "That complex whole which includes knowledge, belief, art, morals, law, custom, and any other capabilities and habits acquired by man as a member of society" (1871:1). His definition soon became famous, and is still much quoted—and mis-quoted, for it is often misunderstood. Writers today often equate his meaning of the term with its meaning among present-day anthropologists, yet the differences are substantial, as the historian George Stocking has shown quite convincingly (1968a:69–109). I discuss the present-day notion of culture with its relativistic implications later. At the moment I focus on the meaning it had for Tylor and his colleagues in order to convey the way in which Victorian thinkers viewed Western civilization within the total gamut of human societies.

The nineteenth-century usage of the term "culture" placed an emphasis on the element of createdness. Institutions like technology, science, law, government, and language were seen as the products of conscious, rational thought, created specifically for the purpose of improving the quality of human life. Culture was also conceived as "artificial," for it was thought to separate us from nature and to set us apart from all other organisms, which necessarily live exclusively in nature. Unlike other creatures, we do not live "in the raw." Only we live in houses with fireplaces for warmth and window panes for light; only we wear manufactured clothes; only we abide by laws and moral rules by which our rights and interests are safeguarded; only we speak by complex languages that enable us to communicate even the most complex thoughts to one another. Civilization (or culture, for the terms were used interchangeably) was conceived as "artificial" in the sense that the Edison light bulb was said to produce artificial light. Just as the Edison bulb took man a step away from nature by giving us control over darkness, so culture has taken man out of nature by making us its master. Artificiality in this sense does not have the connotation of spuriousness or frailty, but rather sophistication and technical excellence, and it can be had in varying degrees. Food that is hunted and cooked over a campfire represents less artificiality than that which is raised on a farm and cooked in an oven. The light given by a campfire is less artificial than that which comes from an electric bulb.

This contrast between life under "natural" conditions and life under the "artificial" conditions of culture is illustrated by the American anthropologist Lewis Henry Morgan. In the earliest period of savagery, he writes, men, like animals, lived by means of "natural subsistence," which is to say that they collected fruits and roots (1877:19–21). Fish subsistence (pp. 21–22) was the next stage, and fish was also "the first kind of artificial food" in that it needed special preparation, to wit, cooking. It was not consumed in its natural state but had to be modified by intelligent effort. What is more, the use of fish liberated man, according to Morgan, for it is a food which is everywhere available, and in unlimited supply—unlike roots, fruit, and even game. By virtue of a fishing economy "mankind became independent of climate and of locality; and by following the shores of the seas and lakes, and the courses of the rivers [they] could, while in the savage state, spread themselves over the greater portion of the earth's surface" (p. 21). Even more independence from nature was achieved by the cultivation of cereals and other plants (pp. 22–24) and by the domestication of animals (pp. 24–26).

The nineteenth-century version of culture (or something very close to it) is still used when we speak of a "cultured person," signifying someone who exhibits refinement, sophistication, and learning. This today is referred to as the humanist meaning of the term. A person is said to be more or less cultured to the extent that he or she is well-informed in the arts, speaks foreign languages (preferably Western European), and exhibits refined manners and tastes. Note that these qualities are artificial in the sense that they have to be cultivated and do not come naturally, though perhaps some assume that the more aristocratic among us find cultivation easier to achieve.

The nineteenth-century anthropological meaning of culture extended the notion of refinement well beyond "high culture"—art, literature, and the like—to all aspects of life, including technology, family organization, religious beliefs, and all other features of civilization. Nineteenth-century anthropologists spoke of societies being more or less cultured: for example, savages whose sexual and marriage practices were thought to be loose or promiscuous, or whose economic arrangements and technology were thought to be crude, were said to be less cultured than we. By this usage, primitive peoples are less refined in their social practices, nearer their natural origins, less elevated by the artificial milieu of culture than more highly civilized peoples. It goes without saying that the people who were thought to be the least cultured were also thought to be the least intelligent and the darkest in pigmentation.

The Victorian British belief in its own (and in the Western world's) superiority has an obvious bearing on the topic of cultural relativism, for this belief is the very antithesis of relativity. What is more, nineteenth-century cultural evolutionism, and the concept of culture that was associated with it, was the antithesis of the relativism that developed in anthropology after the turn of the century. The late nineteenth-century anthropologists were hardly relativists, for they took as indisputable facts that the industrialized countries were the most intelligent in the world, that they therefore had progressed the farthest, and that their institutions were manifestly superior to those of other peoples.

The end of the nineteenth century—specifically, the 1890s—was a period of change among the Western nations; it was also a time of social unrest, economic difficulties, and international instability. These problems in turn had considerable impact on the mood of the Western world and helped to change the intellectual climate that I have described.

Social and economic unrest was linked to the spread of industrialization. As industrial development took place it brought the horrors as well as the benefits of factory work—low wages, long hours, hazardous working conditions, and poor food and housing. It is true that Great Britain passed a number of legislative acts to improve the conditions of labor, regulating working hours, for example, especially of children. Yet the problems were not solved by the end of the century, and besides, other European countries were not as advanced in labor reform. The depression of the 1890s was also very difficult for the worker.

Several international changes were highly unsettling. One change is that Britain was losing its place as the main industrial nation. All of the Western world was rapidly industrializing, but Germany and the United States in particular were threatening to take the lead. Another change was the creation of Germany and Italy. Both of these countries had been fragmented tiny principalities until the second half of the nineteenth century, when each of them underwent a process of political and economic unification and became full-scale nation-states in competition with the other great powers. Germany was also industrializing with much success, and by the end of the century was becoming quite aggressive in its economic and political relations throughout the world. This same aggressiveness helped contribute to World War I.

The 1890s were turbulent and bewildering years for the United States as well as Europe. The American farmer was in trouble—he had been for years—and was now in revolt. His hostility was focused primarily on what he considered the greedy money interests, especially the railroads and banks, and the politicians who were aligned with them. Problems were also severe in the cities, where the laborer worked long hours (when work was available) and was given little pay, and where both living and working conditions were nearly unbearable. The depression of the 1890s was severe—armies of unemployed workers roamed the streets in cities like Chicago, where many survived only by what they could get at soup kitchens. These difficulties stimulated labor movements, including strikes, which were met by armed force supplied by the local and federal governments.

What was happening was that the United States was changing from an agrarian, small-town nation into an urban, industrial one. As industrial development took place, ownership and wealth became concentrated in the hands of a fairly small minority, who became incredibly rich. At the very top were the industrial captains like John D. Rockefeller and Andrew Carnegie, and the financier J. Pierpont Morgan. By contrast, the factory worker in New York City or the farmer in Kansas was forced to live a hard if not an ugly life.

In the 1890s business in America was still looked upon as a wholly private matter; if the public did not like the way the businessman operated, it was felt, its recourse was to avoid his goods or services and then to stand back and watch his business fail. This worked for the corner grocery, so why not with Standard Oil? Yet unlike the grocery, the large corporation could apply leverage to force its way even in spite of public opinion. For example, railroads and manufacturing industries entered into combinations to eliminate competition and to maintain prices. Profits soared for the owners, yet the earnings of the worker remained low. This picture began to change early in the twentieth century, as government assumed a greater regulatory role. But in the 1890s this development was only being glimpsed.

The historian Sidney Pollard (1968:151) summarizes the condition of the Western world toward the end of the nineteenth century; he writes: "it became clear that the social problem had not been solved and there was no sign of a solution; . . . the leading bourgeois nations, having divided the world among themselves, began to feel claustrophobic and turn inward on each other; and . . . a particular phase of history appeared to have run its course." The effect of these developments was to produce a general sense of disillusionment, anger, and frustration; more generally, the effect was a widespread pessimism.

Notice that all the themes and ideas discussed earlier were very optimistic in tone: a purpose or meaning can be found in the universe; the history of life is a history of increasingly better forms, and human beings are the very best of all; human civilization is improving; indeed our own civilization stands at the top of human advancement so far. The new, end-of-the-century pessimism helped change these ideas, or at least to call them into question. For example, how could it seem that the modern world was improving when everything suddenly looked so black? A radically new view of human society and human behavior was emerging in the works of some of the leading thinkers on the Continent, like Freud and Durkheim. This view had it that human beings are not consciously and rationally in control of society, for human affairs are governed by a variety of "irrational" (or at least nonrational) forces, such as unconscious drives and sentiments that have nothing to do with intelligent thinking.

My discussion of the optimistic Victorian ideas focused on Great

Britain, and now I shift to the United States so that I can set the stage for the development of cultural relativism in American anthropology—a development that took place at about the turn of the century and in the context of the new pessimism. The early 1900s in the United States has some bright spots, including a general economic upturn and the appearance of a variety of new and promising inventions—including the automobile and wireless, to name but two. But the mood of pessimism and doubt was very strong nevertheless (see especially Graham 1971:1–51). For example, it was feared by many that the country would come apart at the seams, for deep tensions were felt between the classes and ethnic groups; and confidence in the moral integrity, wisdom and justice of the political order was severely eroded. The economic future of the country also seemed to be in jeopardy. These fears helped stimulate the progressive movement, a great, energetic burst of reform during the early twentieth century, an attempt to bring the country back to a stable course. The pessimism of this era did not suddenly and completely dominate the work of all American writers—the novel in particular seemed not to reflect the sense of dysphoria until about World War I. But by then it was unmistakable. Henry F. May writes: "After 1914 it became increasingly hard to argue that the essential morality of the universe could be shown in the daily course of events. Still more obviously challenged was the special prophetic vision of Social Christianity: the gradual dawn, here on earth, of the kingdom of peace and love" (1959:361).

On the other hand, the effects of the new pessimism were evident in the work of at least some American writers even by the end of the nineteenth century, and they were some of the leading intellectuals in the country. William James was one. He was a Harvard professor and an enormously influential philosopher of the late nineteenth and early twentieth centuries. His philosophy has several parts to it, but most important here was his view of truth: he rejected that we can ever know what is true in an ultimate sense. An idea is "true" if it works satisfactorily, or if it is expedient—if, by believing it to be true, we are better able to deal with a problem. Ideas are evaluated in terms of their usefulness to the thinker. This is the pragmatic test of truth, and James' theory of knowledge goes by the name of pragmatism. What is striking about this theory is its skepticism. The Victorians may have been confident about the findings of science and the wisdom of modern civilization, but not James. The historian Henry Steele Commager writes: "James believed, passionately, that truth was not something that was found, once and for all, but was forever in the making, that it was not single and absolute but plural and contingent" (1950:93).

James was hardly alone in this skepticism, for the nature of scientific knowledge in general was being reassessed. In particular, the notion of scientific laws was changing. The nineteenth-century idea was that scientific laws exist in the real world and are discovered by the scientist, who finds them by looking hard with his instruments and by thinking carefully about what he sees. The twentieth-century view that was emerging is that scientific laws are conventions which human beings manufacture in dealing with the world; laws exist in our minds and not "out there"; they are created and not discovered.

At an even more general level, the idea that a moral purpose or meaning can be found in nature was now called into question. Take the case of man: instead of being the capstone of biological evolution—the supreme creature on earth, the final measure of evolutionary adaptation—we were now seen as an accident. The view was growing that there is nothing necessary in our appearance on earth (and that we may disappear as easily as the Saber-toothed tiger or the dinosaur), and that as creatures go we are not very remarkable. Commager writes:

> The universe unveiled by the new science was illimitable, impersonal, amoral, and incomprehensible. Not only was man's place in the earth evanescent, accidental, and meaningless; the earth itself was but a flyspeck in a universe equally without purpose or meaning. Matter, which had once seemed so unimpeachable, lost its solidity and became in the new physics but a complex of electrical reactions, indistinguishable from pulsating energy. . . . [T]he line between life and death like the line between mind and matter was blurred, and life itself was explained as a convenient but not very accurate term for the chemical process of oxidation. (1950:103)

Commager cites the metaphor "of man as a moth beating his wings with suicidal vanity against the flame" (p. 104).

The same joyless theme was gaining in the literature on American society. For example, American historians were starting to present a rather unflattering account of the Founding Fathers. One of the most influential of these historians was Charles A. Beard, who argued that the way to approach history is not through the lives and deeds of great statesmen and generals, but through interest groups. Economic facts like exploitation make up the basics of any age. Beard made the earlier history look like Fourth of July oratory as he set out to dig beneath appearances and grasp the economic fundamentals. An example—one of his most provocative and well-known works—was a reinterpretation of the American Constitution (1913). The Constitution had been described by several generations of historians as one of the finest manifestations of political theory and high ideals. According to the older interpretation, the French Revolution was a failure, but not the American: we had the high-mindedness and wisdom to draw up a constitutional democracy that resulted in a truly just political order. Beard saw it differently. He wrote a penetrating analysis in which the American Constitution was portrayed as the result of economic interest groups; it was designed specifically to favor one class, certain types of property holders, over others.

Similar developments were taking place in the social sciences, and the economist Thorstein Veblen is illustrative. The son of a Norwegian-born farmer, Veblen was raised on the Wisconsin frontier. He was a very bright young man and impressed his teachers, despite his qualities as a misfit, eventually receiving the Ph.D from Yale. He taught at several major universities during his lifetime, including the University of Chicago, Stanford, the University of Missouri, and the New School for Social Research, and wrote a number of books and articles which reached a wide audience. Veblen's personal alienation was reflected in his economic theory, a main point of which was that the highly optimistic nineteenth-century view of the modern economy was all wrong.

Nineteenth-century economists believed that average, intelligent citizens operate according to the principle of rational self-interest—they behave in such a way as to maximize their material well-being. When faced with a choice, say, between an expensive sweater that is not very warm and an inexpensive one that is, they will buy the cheaper and better one. It was also believed that it is beneficial to society when the individual exercises self-interest in this fashion. For example, by purchasing the cheaper, better sweater, the buyer rewards the businessman who produced it and punishes the one who made the other. The businessman's competitor sees this and tries to manufacture an even superior one at an even cheaper price—and in doing so he lowers the price enough that more people can afford to buy more sweaters, making more jobs for workers, who now have increased buying power to stimulate the production of even more goods of high quality. What is good for business is good for the country.

Veblen argued that this is not the way the system works at all (1899). What motivates the individual and moves the entire system is the barbarian desire to achieve prominence—to be envied. In primitive societies the man who achieves recognition is the one who shows stamina, courage, and fighting prowess, but in modern society it is the accumulation of wealth and its conspicuous consumption or waste that brings notoriety. What motivates the economic system is in truth the very crass desire to be important by being rich, by not having to work, and by living ostentatiously. And the workers are no better than the wealthy, for the poor strive to be like those at the top. They are just as likely to buy the inferior sweater as the other if they feel it will enhance their prestige.

Cultural relativism was another manifestation of the skepticism and pessimism that was growing in America. Relativism denies the social, moral, and intellectual preeminence of Western society: it asserts that our own values, beliefs, and institutions cannot be shown to be better, and that the principle which underlies our position vis-à-vis other societies is the principle of equality.

FURTHER READING

The following are useful for general reading on the historical background discussed in this chapter. Sidney Pollard's *The Idea of Progress* (1968) is a good discussion of the notion of human improvement seen in relation to fluctuations in pessimism and optimism in Western history. Two volumes contain valuable material dealing with Victorian thought: Crane Brinton's *Ideas and Men* (1950: chs. 12 and 13), and the series of essays originally given over the BBC entitled *Ideas and Beliefs of the Victorians* (British Broadcasting Corporation, 1949). Two books that deal with the impact of Darwin and evolution on nineteenth-century thought give very good insight into the intellectual dynamics of Victorian life: Loren Eiseley, *Darwin's Century: Evolution and the Men Who Discovered It* (1961), and John C. Greene, *The Death of Adam: Evolution and Its Impact on Western Thought* (1961). See also the titles cited in the text.

Nineteenth-century anthropology in Britain is the subject of a large literature. For general overviews see Harris, *The Rise of Anthropological Theory* (1968:53–249); Honigmann, *The Development of Anthropological Ideas* (1976:111–60); Voget, *A History of Ethnology* (1975:45–287); and de Waal Malefijt, *Images of Man* (1974:116–59). A few more specialized works are Burrow, *Evolution and Society* (1966); Gruber, "Brixham Cave and the Antiquity of Man" (1965); Hatch, *Theories of Man and Culture* (1973a:13–37); Murphree, "The Evolutionary Anthropologists" (1961); and especially Stocking, *Race, Culture, and Evolution* (1968a:69–132), "Tylor, Edward Burnett" (1968b), "What's in a Name? The Origins of the Royal Anthropological Institute" (1971), and "From Chronology to Ethnology" (1973). For British thought regarding human diversity during the first half of the nineteenth century, see Stocking, "From Chronology to Ethnology: James Cowles Prichard and British Anthropology 1800–1850" (1973).

For late nineteenth- and early twentieth-century developments in Western culture the following are useful: Sidney Pollard, *The Idea of Progress* (1968:ch. 4); Crane Brinton, *Ideas and Men* (1950:ch. 14); and H. Stuart Hughes, *Consciousness and Society* (1958). Four works that deal with these developments in the United States are Henry Steele Commager, *The American Mind* (1950); Otis Graham, *The Great Campaigns* (1971); Richard Hofstadter, *The Age of Reform* (1955); Henry F. May, *The End of American Innocence* (1959); and Morton White, *Social Thought in America* (1957).

CHAPTER THREE

The New Self-Identity

CULTURAL relativism emerged in American anthropology at about the turn of this century as a rather provocative challenge to the old guard by a very small minority within the discipline. This minority grew, however, and by the 1920s it had come to constitute the central core of the profession in this country. As it did so the thesis of relativism enjoyed its fullest flowering in the work of Ruth Benedict and Melville Herskovits. This was no small matter: in 1939 Clyde Kluckhohn expressed a common view among American anthropologists when he described cultural relativism as "probably the most meaningful contribution which anthropological studies have made to general knowledge" (1939:342). In this chapter I show how cultural relativism emerged in American anthropology, and I go into some detail about the way it was conceived by its proponents. The account focuses chiefly on the period before World War II, because a number of fundamental changes took place in the anthropologists' thinking about relativity after the war was over. These changes will be taken up in a later chapter. For now the emphasis is on what may be termed the "classic" phase of cultural relativism.

When modern cultural relativism first appeared in American anthropology early in the century the discipline had already existed in this country for several decades—or longer, depending on the definition used. One convention is to date the discipline from the first appearance of formal organizations devoted to the study of primitive peoples, and by this criterion anthropology got underway in this country in 1842 with the founding of the American Ethnological Society in New York City. The founder, Albert Gallatin, was a wealthy financier and statesman; he served as a Congressman for several years and was Secretary of the Treasury under Jefferson. Gallatin, like Jefferson, had a strong interest in the Indian, and he began the A.E.S. as a forum for scholarly work on the indigenous peoples of America (Bieder 1972:216–304). Similar organizations were started at about the same time in London and Paris in order to focus interest on primitive peoples, suggesting that this development in New York was part of a pattern which extended beyond this country.

Our knowledge of the American Indian was rapidly growing in the nineteenth century, especially in the last half, because of the writings of a number of people who were in direct contact with living Indian tribes and who devoted considerable time and energy to describing them. Among these people were Henry Rowe Schoolcraft (1793–1864), an Indian agent who spoke fluent Ojibwa; Lewis Henry Morgan (1818–1881), an attorney in New York state who became interested in the nearby Iroquois Indians; and John Wesley Powell (1834–1902), head of the Bureau of American Ethnology at the Smithsonian, who made a number of forays into what were then very remote parts of the United States.

At the beginning of the twentieth century, anthropology was organized around several regional centers (Stocking 1968a:277–80), the most important of which were Philadelphia, Washington, Boston, and New York. At each of these, anthropological activities were carried out in connection with either a museum or university, and perhaps with a local anthropological society that held periodic meetings for the purpose of discussing recent findings. The regional activities were dominated by at least one person of local standing, a person who held a university or museum post. The rank and file cohorts consisted of amateurs: attorneys, physicians, businessmen, retired military officers, and the like, who devoted part of their lives to anthropology as an avocation.

The leading center was Washington, and this was dominated by the founder of the Bureau of American Ethnology, John Wesley Powell. The Bureau not only undertook ethnological research on the American Indians but had an active program of publications as well, for the staff included several full-time ethnologists who occasionally conducted their own research and who solicited reports on Indian life from others with an anthropological bent from around the country. Washington also had the preeminent ethnological society in the United States at the time, the Anthropological Society of Washington, which was composed almost entirely of amateur anthropologists.

The turn of the century was a watershed for American anthropology, and at least two important developments were underway (see Stocking 1968a:270–307). First, nineteenth-century evolutionism was seriously challenged. During the last half of the nineteenth century, evolutionism prevailed in anthropological circles in America as in Britain—indeed, one of the leading cultural evolutionary theorists, Lewis Henry Morgan, was an American. But by 1900 a very forceful opposition had emerged, and cultural relativism was a main theme of this opposition. Second, the professionalization of the discipline was underway. Virtually none of the leading figures in nineteenth-century American anthropology had received formal training in the discipline, for the subject was seldom taught in American colleges or universities. For example, Morgan was an attorney, Schoolcraft an Indian agent, and Powell a geologist by training. These people had acquired their anthropological background on their own after establishing other careers. Not only that, but anthropology drew much of its support from people who considered the subject an avocation, the Anthropological Society of Washington being a case in point. Yet by about the turn of the century a movement had begun to transform the field into a fully professional discipline with postgraduate university training as a necessary condition for membership. This made little headway at first, in part because some of the leading anthropologists in the country, notably at the Bureau, drew their support from amateurs and did not want to cut them off. Nevertheless, the movement toward professionalism grew, especially as Ph.D's in anthropology began to appear, mostly from Harvard and Columbia.

These two developments—the assault on evolutionism and the professionalization of the discipline—were related. A main point of the attack on evolutionism was that evolutionary theory was based on shoddy methods; what was needed, it was argued, was to up-grade the discipline by instituting more rigorous, scientific training. In particular, the discipline needed to doff its older, biased, unscientific opinions—opinions, for instance, about our own superiority. One person in particular was associated with both of these developments. This was Franz Boas, who began teaching at Columbia University in 1896, remaining there until he retired in 1937. Boas was born and educated in Germany, holding a doctorate in physics from the University of Kiel. His interests led him gradually to anthropology, and both his Jewish background and left-of-center politics led him to become disillusioned with late nineteenth-century Germany and to seek a career in this country (Stocking 1968a:149–50). By the time he received the appointment at Columbia he had already shifted from physics to anthropology, and his appointment there was as an anthropologist. Boas is especially important here in that he was largely responsible for developing cultural relativism in American anthropology.

Even before the turn of the century Boas began taking graduate students. This was crucial, for as the anthropologists of the older school retired (from the Bureau, for example), and as new jobs were created at universities and museums, Boas' students generally were the ones hired. The controversy between Boas and his followers and the older school were quite heated in the early years of the century, but by the 1920s the Boasians had clearly won the day, if not by the force of their arguments (and the deftness of their politicking within the formal structure of the discipline), then because of the natural attrition of their opponents.

Both the controversy and the eventual victory of the Boasians should be seen from a wider perspective than that of the struggles of a single discipline. This perspective is the changing views about modern civilization and about the nature of the universe in general that were associated with the growing pessimism of the late nineteenth and early twentieth centuries. A reaction was taking place against what Henry F. May calls "the main tenets of traditional American faith" (1959:9), including the beliefs about the moral superiority of Western civilization and about the importance of good manners, taste, and so on. There was growing doubt "that right and wrong were the most important categories, that all good citizens knew one from the other, and that when a choice between them was pointed out the people would act" (1959:28).

The Boasian assault on evolutionism was part of this general intellectual movement, for the attack was directed not only toward the notion of progress, but also toward the traditional beliefs about our moral and cultural superiority and toward the use of our values as absolute standards of judgment. Early in the century Boas argued that anthropology had "rudely shattered some of our cherished illusions" (1908:14). He had already disputed the idea that races must be different in mental ability (Boas 1894): the blacks in Africa and elsewhere could not be assumed to be intellectually inferior to light-skinned people. By early twentieth century he was challenging the superiority of modern civilization itself. He wrote of "the possibility of lines of progress which do not happen to be in accord with the dominant ideas of our own" (1908:26)—which is to say that there may be other criteria for measuring progress than the ones stressed by our own civilization. He argued that our vision is obscured by an emotional, subjective bias "which leads us to ascribe the highest value to that which is near and dear to us" (1904:515). He wrote:

It is somewhat difficult for us to recognize that the value which we attribute to our own civilization is due to the fact that we participate in this civilization, and that it has been controlling all our actions since the time of our birth; but it is certainly conceivable that there may be other civilizations, based perhaps on different traditions and on a different equilibrium of emotion and reason, which are of no less value than ours, although it may be impossible for us to appreciate their values without having grown up under their influence. The general theory of valuation of human activities, as taught by anthropological research, teaches us a higher tolerance than the one which we now profess. (1901:11)

Boas' name belongs on the list of intellectual revolutionaries along with William James, Charles A. Beard, and Thorstein Veblen (see Wagar 1972:10).

Standing firmly in opposition to these revolutionaries were the old-guard champions of the traditional beliefs about the moral and intellectual superiority of Western civilization and about the authority of highbrow taste and refinement. These were the defenders of nineteenth-century certainties. May contends that this old guard continued to control all the strategic centers, including the universities, publishing houses, and the "weightier magazines" like *Harper's* and the *Nation*, until World War I. The anthropological contingent of this old guard—the patriotic evolutionists to whom the American Indian was clearly inferior to the educated and urbane of our own society—was what the relativistic Boas and his followers were pitted against early in the century. May also contends that the overthrow (and conversion) of the traditional champions of American culture came with World War I. This was, in his phrase, the end of American innocence, when the cynics and skeptics prevailed. This was also roughly the time of the Boasian victory, which suggests that the Boasians' success was not due solely to attrition or to their arguments, but was also a reflection of the changing intellectual climate. The Boasians at first had been a vanguard movement, but by World War I the discipline as a whole was catching up.

The argument between the Boasians and evolutionists early in the century commonly took the form of an empirical question: how do we explain the occurrence of very similar or identical cultural traits (like a folktale or a hunting technique) in different parts of the world? Is it due to independent invention, or diffusion? The evolutionists were the defenders of independent invention; in their view when a society reaches a certain point of development the appropriate trait will be invented. More precisely, the mind works according to systematic laws, and as the intellect develops to a slightly higher level it will produce (or invent) the beliefs or practices that are commensurate with its new standing. For example, the principle of justice that prevails among the lower societies is that of a quid pro quo, an eye for an eye and a tooth for a tooth. This principle does indeed help to maintain order, yet there are more efficient ways of doing so, and as the intellect develops, progressively better forms are devised. The highest form is the modern system whereby the injured party is not allowed to take the law into his or her own hands but must allow an impartial system of courts to take charge. As societies develop, they invent systems of justice increasingly like ours, and in doing so they go through a common sequence of stages (Tylor 1881: ch. 16; see Stocking 1968a:105–6).

The Boasians offered a simple critique of the theory of independent invention: the evidence, they argued, indicates that cultural traits are continually diffused from one society to another. A technological device or folktale is transmitted to neighboring tribes by a process of borrowing, and these neighbors then become transmitters of the same trait to more distant societies. Consequently the critical factor in whether or not a people have such a trait as matrilineal clans, nature myths, or a written language is not the state of their intellect, but their position on the map. A tribe living in North America will have different traits from one living in Africa or Asia, and a tribe living in southwestern North America will have different traits from one living in the northeast, regardless of differences in intelligence. The laws of the mind cannot explain the occurrence of cultural items (Boas 1901).

One of the earliest instances of Boas' argument about diffusion vs. independent invention was his rejection of the evolutionists' theory of nature myths, according to which it is a law of human thought that in the lower stages of civilization people explain natural phenomena, like features of the landscape and unusual weather patterns, by reference to mythical figures and supernatural forces. Storms may be explained as manifestations of a deity's anger, and a waterfall as its plaything. Myths or folktales originate when the primitive mind is confronted with the dangers, grandeur, and peculiarities of nature, and they reflect the level of mental development of the simpler peoples. With the advance of civilization these mythical explanations are slowly transformed into scientific ones. Boas' studies of the North American Indians suggested that this explanation was wrong, for by the 1890s it was clear to him that virtually all the myths of a people had been imported from outside. A myth had to originate in somebody's mind, to be sure, yet the origins were lost in the remote past, and Boas reasoned that they could never be retrieved. More important than the occasional invention of a myth (and the generative process of the mind) is the relatively passive acceptance of standard plots that become available through contact with other peoples. Boas argued that the human mind is really quite uncreative, for it works more easily with ready-made items imported from outside than by producing new material from scratch. Local details and emphases are sometimes added to plots that are acquired from others, but these additions usually are not very fundamental. Writing of the folktales of one group of Indian tribes, Boas wrote:

> While dealing with phenomena of nature and with the peculiarities of animals, [these folktales] are not the result of [local] tribal thought; they are at best adaptations of foreign thought, but much more frequently importations that have undergone little if any change. (1898, reprinted in 1966:420–21)

Two years earlier he had written:

> The identity of a great many tales in geographically contiguous areas has led me to the point of view of assuming that wherever considerable similarity between two tales is found in North America, it is more likely to be due to dissemination [or diffusion] than to independent origin. (1896, reprinted in 1966:428)

An implication of Boas' argument is the relativistic notion that the pride of Western society in its own accomplishments is misplaced, for if the cultural features of the American Indian or African tribes cannot be explained by reference to the intellect, neither can ours. Such achievements as writing, tailored clothing, and gunpowder have come to us from various directions by diffusion and are not products of the superior European mind (see Linton 1936: ch. 19).

In rejecting nineteenth-century evolutionism the Boasians were opposing two related matters. First was the pattern of history that the evolutionists thought they had identified, a pattern of advance through time whereby the simpler societies today represent stages that we went through in the past. Second was the evaluation of cultures, according to which those that are lower on the scale are behind us in quality of life, intellectual achievements, and moral development.

The Boasians identified a very different pattern in history, and in doing so they expressed a very different (and relativistic) viewpoint about the evaluation of other peoples. What was the pattern they saw? The first response to come to their minds would have been diffusion (see Lowie 1917:66–97). The history of a culture is one of contact with others and a slow but continuous borrowing of traits. Although it is true that each society can claim to have originated at least a few of the traits in its inventory, the vast majority of traits are acquired from others. To the extent that the Boasians stressed diffusion they rejected that there is a direction in history for, as they conceived it, diffusion is a random process. The borrowing of traits is dependent on such fortuitous matters as whom one has as neighbors, how long the association lasts, and the quality of the relationship.

Yet the Boasians did not think that diffusion told the whole story. Diffusion represented what Boas called an outer force (e.g., 1966:264, 286), but he also spoke of an inner force—which is another matter altogether. This inner force Boas sometimes referred to as the genius of a people, by which he meant their own cultural style, emphasis, or dominating attitudes (e.g., 1966:256). The Kwakiutl Indians, for example, placed a heavy emphasis on the pursuit of social honor, which was expressed in the form of sharp rivalries among kinship groups, whereas modern society stresses economic competition and technological achievement. According to Boas, when traits are received from the outside they tend to be modified and reinterpreted in conformity with the cultural emphasis—cultures are characterized by a tendency toward integration—so the direction that the history of a culture takes is set by the inner cultural genius.

In this sense the Boasians had a very definite idea about direction in history, which is captured by a phrase that was often used, the selectivity of cultures. The Boasians also spoke of cultures as traveling in different directions or exhibiting different emphases (or patterns of integration). For example, Grace de Laguna wrote:

> Cultures have been headed in many different directions and have travelled by different roads to different places. Moreover, each culture has selected its own specific purposes and has set up its own characteristic standards of value. (1942:143)

A critical part of this idea is the stress upon differences. Whereas the evolutionists thought they saw a single direction in history—one of advance—the Boasians saw multiple directions; each culture has its own unique pattern of advance and is pursuing its own goals.

The principle of the selectivity of cultures is illustrated by one of the first textbooks by an American anthropologist. This appeared in 1922 and was written by Alexander Goldenweiser, a student of Boas who received a Ph.D. from Columbia in 1910. Starting with the Eskimo, Goldenweiser described several societies in his book in an attempt to give the student a brief sample of what other cultures are like (1922:31–128). He remarked that the Eskimo achieved a near-perfect adjustment in the economic and technological sphere, for they developed an ingenious system of artifacts and techniques which enabled them to survive in a difficult environment, yet they virtually ignored other spheres of cultural activity, including social organization, which is "exceedingly simple and amorphic." For instance, they lack formal political leaders and have no clan system. Their art has achieved excellence in a few areas, especially bone carving and engraving, but otherwise it is undeveloped. Among the Northwest Coast peoples what stands out is the wood industry, such as the elaborately carved boxes and "totem poles." Among the Iroquois the sociopolitical organization is emphasized, for these people elaborated a very complex political system based on matrilineal clanship. In Australia the "economico-industrial phase" is little developed (it is "simple and crude") but the "socio-ceremonial side," the complex system of kinship and religious rituals, "is highly elaborated." Goldenweiser wrote:

> The historic fate of [these] groups have evidently been individual and particular and have driven them in directions that may here and there have reached corresponding levels, without however lying along the same line of advance. . . . From the comparison of the separate aspects of [these] civilizations it appears that these . . . have followed lines of development that were essentially disparate. (1922:127)

Each of these societies has emphasized a different aspect of culture and has developed in that direction.

Ruth Benedict was another student of Boas, and her *Patterns of Culture*, published in 1934, is perhaps the best-known instance of the thesis about the selectivity of cultures. She wrote that other peoples virtually ignore some spheres of life that to us seem crucial, whereas they may elaborate a particular trait to such an extent that to us it seems fantastic (p. 23). She asks us to imagine:

a great arc on which are ranged the possible interests provided either by the human age-cycle or by the environment or by man's various activities. A culture that capitalized even a considerable proportion of these would be as unintelligible as a language that used all the clicks, all the glottal stops, all the labials, dentals, sibilants, and gutterals from voiceless to voiced and from oral to nasal. Its identity as a culture depends upon the selection of some segments of this arc. Every human society everywhere has made such selection in its cultural institutions. Each from the point of view of another ignores fundamentals and exploits irrelevancies. One culture hardly recognizes monetary values; another has made them fundamental in every field of behaviour. In one society technology is unbelievably slighted even in those aspects of life which seem necessary to ensure survival; in another, equally simple, technological achievements are complex and fitted with admirable nicety to the situation. One builds an enormous cultural superstructure upon adolescence, one upon death, one upon after-life. (p. 24)

Melville Herskovits' idea of cultural focus is another instance of the Boasian concept of the selectivity of cultures. By cultural focus Herskovits meant that sphere of culture which has become the center of attention among a people and which has been elaborated by them. Herskovits described the cultural focus as

the tendency of every culture to exhibit greater complexity, greater variation in the institutions of some of its aspects than in others. So striking is this tendency to develop certain phases of life, while others remain in the background, so to speak, that in the shorthand of the disciplines that study human societies these focal aspects are often used to characterize whole cultures. (1947:542)

Why does one society choose to emphasize one feature and not others? It is a matter of historical accident. A culture might have a slight inclination in a certain direction, and contact with another people might help emphasize that development. Once the process has begun it tends to continue as more and more of the cultural inventory is molded and reinterpreted in conformity with the emerging theme. Ralph Linton remarked that it is an unanswerable question why cultures happen to select the orientations they do: "In each of these cases there was a fixation of interest, but the causes of this fixation must have been highly complex and in large measure accidental." Whatever the cause, he continued, once the cultural interests become fixed they are "of overwhelming importance to the culture configuration, molding the other elements within it to serve the ends which they indicated as desirable" (1936:463).

The Boasians viewed the evolutionary schemes of the nineteenth century as mere conjectures, flights of the imagination that went far beyond the limits of the data, yet the selectivity of cultures to them was a demonstrable fact that had grown out of the empirical evidence itself. The Boasians had the self-image of serious fieldworkers, trained in the most rigorous methods; they had gone to live among the Kwakiutl, Comanche, and Pueblos, and could report the differences in cultural genius as scientific observations of fact. A later generation of anthropologists would dispute this finding—and they would raise serious doubts about the scientific standards of Boasian field research. But this reaction did not come until well into the 1930s, and it did not reach maturity until after World War II.

Nor was this finding about the selectivity of cultures insignificant in the Boasian view, for it constituted a framework for viewing cultural differences. What is crucial in distinguishing one society from another is not that the members of the one are brighter, or that they live in a different environment, or that they are members of a different race with different propensities; it is rather that their culture is traveling in a different direction.

The pattern in history that the Boasians had identified expressed a form of cultural relativism. To say that cultures travel in different directions is to say that each has different values, for it is the cultural values which provide the ends or goals that are sought and the directions in history. Iroquois culture contained a value concerning political organization that was lacking among the Eskimo, for instance. What is more, values are historically conditioned: they reflect the variable and often fortuitous circumstances of the past and are not a matter of necessity, are not grounded in logical, material, or moral requirements. This means that any hierarchical evaluation of cultures like that which the evolutionists proposed is invalid. Societies cannot be ranked relative to one another because there are no criteria—or values—that transcend cultural boundaries. It would be a fundamental error, say, to evaluate the Eskimo as inferior to the Iroquois simply because the former did not place an emphasis on political development. Nor is it legitimate to rank the Australian aborigines below modern civilization on the basis of technological achievements, a sphere of culture that we value, not they.

Whereas the evolutionists were thought to lack objectivity in that they used their own cultural values as universal standards, Boasian relativism was conceived as a manifestation of scientific detachment because of its rigid exclusion of value judgments. Benedict remarked (1934a:3–4) that in science in general there can be "no preferential weighting" given to the objects of its inquiry, in that the scientist's personal values must not be allowed to make some phenomena seem more important than they are. In the study of cactuses, termites, or the nebulae, for example, all forms are given equal significance. But in the study of mankind "one local variation, that of Western civilization," has been assigned a position of superiority by the social sciences. Anthropology could not properly develop as long as it continued to evaluate its own way of life as higher than others, or "as long as these distinctions between ourselves and the primitive, ourselves and the barbarian, ourselves and the pagan, held sway over people's minds."

The relationship between the selectivity of cultures and cultural relativism emerges quite clearly in a discussion of Melville Herskovits on the meaning of the terms primitive and savage (1955, reprinted in 1973:26–27). Herskovits remarked that the Australian aborigines are customarily considered to be among the most primitive peoples on earth, and yet their kinship system is "so complex that for many years it defied the attempts of students to analyze it." It puts our own system to shame, for "we do not even distinguish between paternal and maternal grandparents, or older or younger brother, and call literally dozens of relatives by the same word, 'cousin.' " If we define "primitive" by criteria that would be meaningful to the Australians—by reference to the values of kinship—then modern Western society ranks low, Australian society high.

Yet Western society has brought about its political and economic dominance throughout the world. Does this not constitute an objective criterion for judging our superiority? Nowhere do we find Australian aborigines establishing laws, working conditions, or hospitals for European whites. Herskovits noted that Europeans, and later Americans, achieved supremacy over other cultures because of a technological apparatus—especially weaponry (1961, in 1973:156–58). Within the sphere of technological achievement we can easily claim superiority. Yet this does not mean that we are superior in other areas like social organization, political structure, art, or religion. What is more, even our technological supremacy needs to be qualified, for within that sphere of culture "questions of better or worse cannot be resolved unless we disregard all but purely technical considerations." In other words, it is a simple and obvious point that a gun is more effective than a spear. But more than technological values are involved in deciding to what use the technology is put: who is to say that political and economic expansion are worth the effort?

In this passage Herskovits acknowledged that in the sphere of technology a general cross-cultural standard of judgment can indeed be found. Here at least was one concession among pre-World War II Boasian anthropologists about the relativity of values. Another Boasian anthropologist, Robert H. Lowie, illustrates this point in greater detail. Lowie remarked that "tools are contrivances for definite practical purposes," and as such they can be judged by how well they do the job (1920:438). "Hence it is a purely objective judgment that metal axes are superior to those of stone." It is an equally objective judgment that the domestication of animals is an advance over hunting as a form of subsistence. Here we may speak of "*progressive* change" (the emphasis is Lowie's). What is more, he suggests, the historical record for material culture exhibits a pattern of advance through time: "At least in material culture and in sheer knowledge there has been a steady gain" throughout human history (1929:294–95). The principle that underlies this advance is that once an economically advantageous development has occurred it is not likely to be forgotten or discarded.

On the other hand, Lowie is clear that advances of this kind are not consciously and rationally sought, as the Victorian anthropologists believed, so the desire for material improvement is not a force that impinges upon or restricts the selectivity of cultures. It is not a value that all people share or that guides the development of their cultures. He noted the case of the Tierra del Fuegans who lived in conditions of nearly unbearable cold and who had never devised the kind of clothing that would protect them: "Men and women often went naked and at best wore a cape of stiff seal or otter skin extending to the waist" (1929:19–20). Similarly, the Indians of the Gran Chaco lived in grass huts which gave little protection in a downpour. The Athabaskans of Canada had nothing more than "a miserable tent or lean-to" for protection against the elements, whereas tribes related to them and living in much more pleasant climates to the south "enjoy[ed] warm underground houses." Material adaptation is a cultural goal only if it is selected by the vicissitudes of history.

The link between the selectivity of cultures and cultural relativism has an important corollary. If the one is an established, empirical fact, so is the other. The Boasians did not doubt the validity of the selectivity of cultures, and consequently they saw cultural relativism as an established fact as well. Herskovits wrote that cultural relativism "represents a scientific, inductive attack on an age-old philosophic problem, using fresh, cross-cultural data, hitherto not available to scholars, gained from the study of the underlying value-systems of societies having the most diverse customs" (1955, in 1973:4). He suggested that cultural relativism came about as a result "of the massive ethnographic documentation gathered by anthropologists" (1951, in 1973:39), and that "it took many years of field work to establish it" (1956, in 1973:90).

Two points can be made about Herskovits' notion of the factual basis of cultural relativism. First, he removed relativism from the sphere of philosophy and placed it in the domain of science, for he suggested that it is not an issue that will be resolved by deductive reasoning or the logical analysis of premises. Rather, it is an empirical matter that can be resolved by hard data. This is a question that will come up again. Second, Herskovits was offering a historical explanation of how and why cultural relativism came about in American anthropology, and Franz Boas plays an important role in this explanation. When Boas turned from physics to anthropology he focused heavily on field research in his work, and he insisted that his students do so as well. For him the physicist's research is in the laboratory, but the anthropologist's is in the field and amounts to gathering ethnographic data. Nineteenth-century evolutionists would not have agreed: to them a major research activity was to locate evolutionary patterns by sifting the data collected by others, and this took place in the study. Boas' equation of fieldwork and research was tied to his efforts to upgrade and professionalize the discipline, for in his mind if anthropology was to become a genuinely rigorous science, anthropologists would have to stop speculating and go to the field. According to Herskovits, once the anthropologists left the comforts of the study and confronted the variability of cultures firsthand, cultural relativism was an unavoidable result.

Herskovits' explanation does not adequately recognize the fieldwork that was done in the nineteenth century. Why did the work of School-craft or Morgan not force cultural relativism onto the discipline's consciousness? Relativism may have received a strong boost with Boasian field research, yet more important is that fieldwork now was under-taken in an intellectual climate that was radically different—a climate of skepticism. It is to the intellectual milieu and not to the Boasian demands about research that we should look in understanding the roots of cultural relativism. It is paradoxical that my argument here is more relativistic than Herskovits'. Herskovits suggested that relativism was forced on us by the data, whereas my argument is that it is historically conditioned: it is rooted in the intellectual climate of a particular time and place.

My historical explanation of relativism raises a crucial issue that will reappear in several places in this book, and it is appropriate to mention it here as an aside. It is tempting to think that if such anthropological ideas as cultural relativism are historically conditioned, then they do not exhibit a pattern of advance or progress. An idea such as relativism would simply be a fortuitous product of its time, incommensurate with and no better than the views it replaced. One caveat: if this were so, the purpose of this book would be undermined, for why discuss the sequence of changes in and the logical structure of a set of ideas if they go nowhere? In the next chapter I will suggest that the cultural relativism of the Boasians truly was a signal development, but for now I want to avoid specifics and to make the general point that, however Boasian relativism may have come about, it provided a reasonable solution to certain moral difficulties associated with the Victorian point of view: in relation to those difficulties, the Boasian perspective may be construed as an improvement. We shall see that Boasian relativism was also flawed, and that it was eventually challenged and changed, but in the present context that is beside the point. What is important here is that to accept a historical explanation of a set of ideas is not to deny the possibility of evaluating those ideas. The difficulties of Victorian thought were fundamental ones and can be judged by standards that transcend the historical moment. Looking back in time, one can hardly help feeling sympathetic with the changes the Boasians made; if forced to choose, it would be difficult not to take Boasian relativism over the other point of view.

Of course it can be argued that such sympathy for the Boasians reflects the intellectual climate of one's own age, or that the standards we use in assessing the Boasians are historically conditioned. Yet the fact that we must use a historically conditioned, cultural perspective in viewing the Boasian (or any other) system of thought does not negate our own critical faculties—we may use our cultural perspective intelligently and critically. Nor does it negate the possibility that we may arrive at a standard of judgment that has a reasonable claim to validity beyond the limits of our own time and culture.

So far I have shown that the cultural relativism that emerged in American anthropology was associated with two somewhat different parts of Boasian thought. First, diffusionism as it was conceived by Boas and his followers implied that Western people cannot take full credit for their accomplishments since a very large share of their cultural inventory came to them from other societies. Second, the principle of the selectivity of cultures carried the implication that our notions of progress and achievement do not constitute absolute standards of judgment since they reflect our own cultural preferences. A third feature of Boasian thought was also involved in the new cultural relativism, and this differs from the other two in that it is a far more subtle matter, perhaps in the long run it is the most important of the three, and it was something that the Boasians were not fully aware of. It is that the term "culture" had undergone a very significant change in meaning. I will not try to explain how the change came about or why it was so little understood by the very people who were involved in it (see Stocking 1968a:133–307 and Hatch 1973a:13–73); but I do need to describe what the change was and how it relates to the new cultural relativism.

The crux of the change was this: the critical element of culture as the term was used by the Victorian anthropologists was intelligence, whereas to the Boasians it was learning. To nineteenth-century cultural evolutionists, the artificial cultural milieu in which human beings live is a more or less conscious creation of rational minds. When faced with a need, say, to secure protection from cold and damp weather, the mind devises a solution. This version of culture did not deny the importance of learning, of course. It was assumed that children should go to school to become well educated and to enjoy civilization to its fullest. There is no need for each generation to re-discover what others already knew. Yet in the final analysis, learning itself was thought to be a matter of intelligence. Children may be taught things at school that they would not invent on their own (such as the concept of zero), but once these subjects are presented, the youngsters accept them because they have the good sense to see their usefulness and value.

The twentieth-century Boasian view of culture construed learning very differently. At least two innovations underlay this difference, the first of which is that learning was now thought to be as much a matter of emotion as reason. However rational and sensible our beliefs and practices may be, according to Boas, once learned we have an emotional attachment to them, so that an important accompaniment of all learning is a strong devotion to the patterns that are acquired. Boas made this point by saying that cultural beliefs and practices have emotional associations, in that deviations become intolerable to the members of society (e.g., Boas 1938:204–225). Clyde Kluckhohn, a Harvard anthropologist and one of Boas' most articulate followers, wrote:

> Once . . . a way of handling a situation becomes institutionalized, there is ordinarily great resistance to change or deviation. When we speak of "our sacred beliefs," we mean of course that they are beyond criticism and that the person who suggests modification or abandonment must be punished. No person is emotionally indifferent to his culture. Certain cultural premises may become totally out of accord with a new factual situation. Leaders may recognize this and reject the old ways in theory. Yet their emotional loyalty continues in the face of reason because of the intimate conditionings of early childhood. (1949:26)

The second innovation underlying the new version of culture was the notion of the unconscious, or more accurately of unconscious patterns or processes. Nineteenth-century anthropologists operated largely without the idea of an unconscious dimension to human behavior. If they had given any thought to the matter they would have said that the process of learning takes place at the conscious level, or that people *think* when learning: little or nothing enters the mind unless it passes through the conscious intellect. Similarly, culture consists of ideas and practices that are held at the level of conscious thought, so in principle it should be possible to elicit a culture in its entirety simply by asking people to describe their way of life. It would not have occurred to Victorian anthropologists that they needed subtle techniques for eliciting deep-seated patterns that are beyond people's awareness. Boas was one of a number of turn-of-the century writers who helped changed this (see Hughes 1958; and Hatch 1973a:37–40, 50–57, 65–71). In his view customs are habitual patterns of thought and behavior (most of which we learn as children), and once we acquire them they become "automatic" and "unreflective," like the rules of grammar. He did not necessarily imply the existence of an unconscious system in the modern sense, but he was clear that much of what goes on in human behavior springs not from conscious thought, but from obscure patterns in the mind.

Boas' view of the unconscious seems to have been that of a bundle of discrete, learned patterns, including grammatical rules, mythical plots, modes of etiquette, and principles of artistic design, among others. By and large his work lacks the notion of unconscious personality structure and dynamics, such as appears in Freudian theory. The primary unconscious dynamic that Boas identified was that of consistency: in his view there is a general tendency for the mind to work toward some degree of consistency among the patterns it contains.

By culture the Victorian anthropologists meant rational creations. To the Boasians, culture is made up largely of unconscious and emotional patterns—such as patterns of dress or etiquette—that we hardly recognize we have but which we feel very strongly about if violated. The emotional reaction we experience when we see someone on the street with garish or ill-fitting clothes (or no clothes at all) or when at a restaurant we observe someone accidentally knocking over water glasses and spilling food has nothing to do with reason and intelligence. To the Boasians most of an individual's behavior is an expression of just this sort of unconscious and emotional pattern: this is the most important part of the human character in that it explains a large share of what we do, and most of the inventory of a culture is made up of patterns of this kind. What is more, Victorian anthropologists hardly knew it existed. Their notion of culture was almost completely devoid of what to the Boasians was the most important part.

The Boasians did not eliminate the conscious and rational dimension altogether from either the human character or from culture, yet human rationality was now construed very differently. To Victorian anthropologists, the chief limitation on rational thought was intelligence. Lesser minds do not see the implications, say, of lazy behavior or dishonesty; they do not think matters through, whereas the very bright among us can arrive at both truth and a happier existence by the sheer power of intellect. To Boas, however, rational thought processes are limited more by the emotional and unconscious patterns of culture than by intelligence (Hatch 1973a:54–56). Take the reasons we give for behaving as we do. Victorian anthropologists like Tylor or Spencer could offer sensible justifications for virtually all they did— why they ate with knives and forks, wore shoes and hats, and took Sundays off. Yet Boas saw these "reasons" as after-the-fact rationalizations; they justify behavior patterns that in truth are not rational at all but customary. Victorian anthropologists erred in believing their own fabrications.

The area of life where reason would seem to be the most unencumbered by emotional and unconscious patterns is science, yet here too the intellect is hardly free, according to Boas. For instance, even the scientist becomes attached to his or her theories and resists giving them up in the face of contrary evidence (Boas 1938:224). In this sense the intellectual life is never divorced from the emotional. In addition, patterns of a different order—namely, unconscious, cognitive patterns of thought—also influence the way the scientist sees the world. Linguistic patterns are an example. Grammatical forms, like tense and mood, structure the way the scientist thinks and perceives, and they do so in a way that escapes notice. It follows that very subtle differences—and perhaps sometimes very major ones—exist in the way different language speakers analyze the world. Cultural assumptions and world view also influence the observations of even the most critical observer.

In 1917 Alfred Kroeber, one of Boas' most prolific and influential students, published an article in which the role of culture in human thought and behavior was spelled out in detail. A main theme of the article is that an important difference separates behavior which is organic from that which is cultural or superorganic, and to illustrate he compared the speech of dogs and cats with human beings. On the surface the speech forms seem very much alike, Kroeber says, yet they are not at all. If a puppy is raised with a litter of kittens and has no contact with other dogs it will still have canine vocal patterns. It will bark and growl and not meow or hiss. If its toe is stepped on it will whine like a dog and not squeal like a cat. When it hears another dog's bark for the first time it will respond as one dog to another and not as a cat. Kroeber writes that "dog speech is as ineradicably part of dog nature, as fully contained in it without training or culture, as wholly part of the dog organism, as are teeth or feet or stomach or motions or instincts" (p. 170). Dog speech is inborn or organic. By contrast, if an English infant—born of a long line of English speakers—were transported at birth to Central Africa and raised by Bantu speakers, he will not speak English but will be perfectly fluent in the Bantu tongue of his adopted parents. Nor will he find it easier to learn English as an adult than other native Bantu speakers. To Kroeber, language is learned and is not inborn; like the rest of culture, it is "superorganic."

To an extent Tylor and other nineteenth-century cultural evolutionists would have agreed with Kroeber's argument about language. According to Tylor, people everywhere have passed beyond the level of self-evident sounds and gestures in their speech patterns and communicate by conventional linguistic forms. The reason is that the self-evident mode of speech (like shivering to suggest it is cold) is not efficient or precise enough for everyday needs, consequently it is modified here and there in order to improve communication (see Tylor 1881: chs. 4–5). Since these improvements have to be learned, an English child raised in Bantu-speaking Africa would indeed speak Bantu, not English, and would not automatically understand English words or expressions the first time he heard them. Yet Tylor would also have argued that English is a more developed language than any of the Bantu tongues—it is more precise and better able to express abstract thoughts, and it is developed farther beyond the level of self-evident sounds. What is more, he assumed that the typical native African is not as intelligent as the typical Englishman. In his view, the British child raised in Africa, being from a more intelligent stock, would be able to learn English more quickly and completely than other Africans, for English is more perfectly suited to his intellect.

Tylor and Kroeber would have disagreed on another matter concerning language, in that Kroeber gave greater recognition to the unconscious nature of linguistic patterns—grammatical and phonemic rules. To Kroeber, a very large part of any language (its structural rules) is beyond the level of conscious awareness and is absorbed by the child without his or her knowledge, and the burden of linguistic analysis is to ferret out these unconscious patterns. By contrast, Tylor viewed language primarily as a conscious process. An example is his discussion about the repetitiveness of primitive languages. All languages have some repetitiveness; in English for instance the verb must agree with the subject, and in this sense it "repeats" the subject. Tylor believed that repetitiveness of this kind is far more pronounced in primitive tongues. The tense of the verb or the gender of the subject (or whatever) is repeated again and again in word forms throughout the utterance. Why? To help both speaker and listener remember what is being said. These are primitive people with less developed minds than ours and they need such helpful devices when they communicate. Linguistic repetitiveness, he noted, "makes it clear to the dullest hearer" what is being said (1881:148). Such repetitiveness is fully developed "among the barbarians of Africa," whereas it "has mostly disappeared" from "the languages of modern Europe, especially our own"; he suggested that its near-disappearance among Europeans is "probably because with the advance of intelligence it was no longer found necessary" (1881:150). To Tylor it is to the conscious intellect and not to the unconscious that we look in understanding the patterns of language.

This difference between Kroeber and Tylor had bearing on the matter of language acquisition. Tylor's view of speech implied that the important factor in learning another language is intelligence. In principle it should be easier for the civilized European to learn the tongue of the savage Tierra del Fuegan or Hottentot than for them to learn ours. To Kroeber all languages include a large body of grammatical forms that are held at the unconscious level. Civilized Europeans have the same hurdle to cross in learning the speech of the Tierra del Fuegan or Hottentot as the latter have in learning English or French.

Kroeber's article on "The Superorganic" also contained a classic argument about the role of the great man or genius in history: to what extent are the true achievements of mankind, like major inventions, discoveries, or political conquests, due to the unusual abilities of specific individuals, or geniuses? Kroeber agreed that there are congenital differences among individuals and that some men and women are more likely than others to be the ones to change the course of history by the force of their intellects. Yet genius operates in a context of cultural ideas and forces that are even more important. He wrote that an "invention or discovery springs in no way from the make-up of the great man, or that of his ancestors, but is a product of the civilization into which he with millions of others is born" (p. 196).

The expression of genius is largely a matter of social forces. Kroeber allows that Charles Darwin had considerable mental ability, but if Darwin were born sooner, or in some other society, he would not have arrived at the principle of natural selection. He could not have, because the cultural ideas that he needed to work with were not there. What is more, if he were born later, someone else would have come up with the theory already, since its appearance was inevitable given the intellectual developments that were taking place in Western society at the time. As a matter of fact, another person, Wallace, had arrived at the idea of natural selection at nearly the same time as Darwin and could easily have been the first to publish. Kroeber cites a series of simultaneous discoveries to substantiate his case about the inevitability of inventions. For example, the telephone was invented and oxygen was discovered by several people separately. The same was true of the nebular hypothesis, the prediction of the existence of Neptune, the inventions of the steamboat, telephone, and photography. The list goes on and on. Kroeber wrote that discoveries are "not directly contingent upon the personality of the actual inventors . . . but would have been made without them" (p. 201).

The implication of Kroeber's discussion of genius is that the individual is not an autonomous agent, freely creating and innovating according to native intellect and ability. We all operate within a cultural milieu that plays an enormous role in how and what we think.

Earlier I said that the term "culture" had a different meaning among Victorian anthropologists from what it had among the Boasians. Boas in particular changed the culture concept radically, and it is essentially his meaning that prevails today. If a random sample of living anthropologists were asked to give one main attribute of culture, the most frequent response would be that it plays a major role in shaping thought and behavior. This is a topic that occupies a prominent spot surely in nearly every introductory cultural anthropology course in the country. Yet that topic would have made little sense to a Victorian anthropologist, to whom *reason* governs behavior, and to whom culture is simply the rational practices that have been devised in the course of history. To explain to Tylor or Morgan what is meant today by the statement that culture influences behavior would require an elaborate explanation; to explain what is meant today by "culture" would be tantamount to translating a cognate word from one language into another.

The implications of the new meaning of culture for cultural relativism are considerable. Thought processes always take place in a cultural medium, which is in part emotional (or value-laden), and which at any rate is largely beyond our awareness. We always perceive—and judge—from a cultural point of view, and our perceptions and judgments are therefore relative to that point of view.

Boasian relativism was a crucial matter. It was not quite as spectacular a development perhaps as the Copernican revolution, which changed the medieval idea that the earth is at the center of the heavens: Copernicus contributed to a fundamental re-definition of the place that man occupies in the universe, for his theory of the solar system carried the implication that neither the earth nor humanity has the cosmic importance that had traditionally been assigned to them. Boas' contribution was parallel and nearly as momentous: Boasian relativism carried the implication that modern civilization does not have the importance that it thought it had. Here was a fundamental re-definition of where we stand in the world. An index of the new self-image was the Boasian reaction against the terms "savage" and "primitive"; these were explicitly eliminated from the anthropologist's lexicon, for they implied the cultural hierarchy that the Boasians rejected. In place of the terms "savage" and "civilized" the Boasians preferred to speak simply of "cultures," a term which in their minds carried no implication of superiority or inferiority.

FURTHER READING

The main sources for Benedict's relativism are her *Patterns of Culture* (1934a) and "Anthropology and the Abnormal" (1934b). The main writings by Herskovits on cultural relativism have been brought together and published in his *Cultural Relativism* (1973). Herskovits' writings on this topic are somewhat anachronistic, for they appeared primarily after World War II. Nevertheless, his ideas came to maturity before the war and his views about relativism were far more in keeping with anthropological thought of the 1930's than later.

Some useful works on nineteenth-century American anthropology are Robert Bieder, "The American Indian and the Development of Anthropological Thought in the United States, 1780–1851" (1972); the essays by Bieder and Thomas Tax in a volume edited by Timothy Thoresen entitled *Toward a Science of Man: Essays in the History of Anthropology* (1975); Curtis Hinsley, "Amateurs and Professionals in Washington Anthropology, 1879–1903" (1976); Jacob Gruber, "Horatio Hale and the Development of American Anthropology" (1967); A. I. Hallowell, "The Beginnings of Anthropology in America" (1960); Regna Darnell, "Daniel Brinton and the Professionalization of American Anthropology" (1976); Neil M. Judd, *The Bureau of American Ethnology* (1967); and Nancy Oestreich Lurie, "Women in Early American Anthropology" (in Helm, ed., 1966). Very rich material on late nineteenth-century American anthropology is scattered through George Stocking's *Race, Culture, and Evolution* (1968a).

For turn-of-the-century developments in American anthropology two works in particular stand out. First is Stocking's *Race, Culture and Evolution* (1968a), although the material is scattered over several chapters. Second is Regna Darnell's Ph.D. dissertation, "The Development of American Anthropology, 1880–1920: From the Bureau of American Ethnology to Franz Boas" (1969).

A large literature exists on Boasian anthropology, although it is of very uneven quality. The place to start is three articles by George Stocking: "The Scientific Reaction Against Cultural Anthropology, 1917–1920" (in Stocking 1968a), and "The Basic Assumptions of Boasian Anthropology" (in Stocking 1974), and "Ideas and Institutions in American Anthropology" (Stocking 1976). Other discussions (and further references) are found in: Marvin Harris, *The Rise of Anthropological Theory* (1968:250–421); Elvin Hatch, *Theories of Man and Culture* (1973a:37–161); John J. Honigmann, *The Development of Anthropological Ideas* (1976:192–231); Fred W. Voget, A *History of Ethnology* (1975:317–39, 361–83, 402–25); and Annemarie de Waal Malefijt, *Images of Man: A History of Anthropological Thought* (1974:215–55).

CHAPTER FOUR

The Call for Tolerance

I N the preceding two chapters I wrote in the historical mode, and now I switch to the philosophical. My purpose is to look closely at ethical relativism in order to ask if it is sound. To the Boasians of course it was more than that: to them it was inescapable, a moral philosophy that both empirical fact and good sense command us to accept. Yet we are led to wonder by a striking pattern in the literature on the subject. By and large ethical relativists have been anthropologists and not philosophers, and it is chiefly in the anthropological literature that we find arguments in its favor. Two people in particular have stood out as its proponents in the United States, Melville Herskovits and Ruth Benedict, both of whom were students of Boas.* Almost without exception, the philosophers are disapproving, for usually they mention ethical relativism only to criticize it while in the course of arguing some other ethical theory.

At least two very different versions of ethical relativism have been advanced by anthropologists, and these need to be distinguished since they have their own faults and virtues. The first is sometimes classified (erroneously, as we shall see) as a form of skepticism, and I will call it the Boasian version of ethical relativism. This is the "classic" form of relativism in American anthropology that was described in chapter 3, one that enjoyed considerable prestige among anthropologists on

---

* One could add William Graham Sumner, the Yale sociologist, to the list of leading writers on ethical relativism; see his *Folkways* (1906). If we go beyond the borders of the United States, a fourth name should be added, that of Edward Westermark, an anthropologist at the University of London during most of his career; see his *Ethical Relativity* (1932).

this side of the Atlantic in the years before World War II. Skepticism in ethics is the view that nothing is really either right or wrong, or that there are no moral principles with a reasonable claim to legitimacy. It has been suggested that the Boasian position differs from this on one main point: Boasian relativism implies that principles of right and wrong do have some validity, but a very limited one, for they are legitimate only for the members of the society in which they are found (Ladd 1973:9). The values of the American middle class are valid for middle-class Americans, but not for the Trobriand Islanders, and vice versa.

Philosophers have presented a wide range of arguments against Boasian ethical relativism, some more telling than others, and they tend to follow a logical progression. Taking the criticisms in order, the first attacks the Boasian belief that its ethical relativism is dispassionately objective, or that it excludes value judgments in assessing other people. According to this argument, Boasian relativism is in essence a moral theory that gives a central place to one particular value. Frank Hartung comments that ethical relativism "is flying under false colors," for although "it claims to be objective," in truth it "is surreptitiously moral" (1954:118). It contains a more or less implicit value judgment in its call for tolerance: it asserts that we *ought* to respect other ways of life. The Boasians claimed to view cultural differences in the same dispassionate way that the chemist regards differences among molecules, yet the chemist would have no moral qualms about manipulating or suppressing the properties of certain elements. By contrast, Herskovits wrote: "The very core of cultural relativism is the social discipline that comes of respect for differences—of mutual respect. Emphasis on the worth of many ways of life, not one, is an affirmation of the values in each culture" (1955, reprinted 1973:33).

Boasian ethical relativism is not a form of skepticism at all, strictly speaking, for it does not assert that there is no general standard of value. Rather, it supplies such a standard, one that should be adhered to in all societies. Presumably the Navajo, Trobrianders, and Samoans should be just as tolerant of others as should middle-class Americans; conversely, they, like Americans, can be judged for their intolerance. Herskovits remarked that tolerance is not to be unilateral (1956, in

1973:94); not only should we show respect for cultural differences, but others should do so as well.

The issue of tolerance was a major feature of Boasian thought—without it the question of relativism would have seemed somewhat trivial or esoteric. The supposed "fact" of the cultural variability of values, in itself, is not much more than an interesting datum, like the fact that butterflies differ in color; the tendency for nineteenth-century evolutionists to allow their cultural biases to influence their work, and the Boasian ability to rise above their prejudices, is but a matter of professional maturity. But the call for tolerance was an appeal to the liberal philosophy regarding human rights and self-determinism. It expressed the principle that others ought to be able to conduct their affairs as they see fit, which includes living their lives according to the cultural values and beliefs of their society. Put simply, what was at issue was human freedom.

The call for tolerance (or for the freedom of foreign peoples to live as they choose) was a matter of immediate, practical importance in light of the pattern of Western expansion. As Western Europeans established colonies and assumed power over more and more of the globe, they typically wanted both to Christianize and civilize the indigenous peoples. Christian rituals were fostered or imposed, and "pagan" practices were prohibited, sometimes with force. The practice of plural marriage was condemned as a barbaric custom, and Western standards of modesty were enforced in an attempt to improve morals by covering the body. In the Southwest of North America, Indians who traditionally had lived in scattered encampments were made to settle in proper villages like "civilized" people. The treatment of non-Western societies by the expanding nations of the West is a very large blot on our history, and had the Boasian call for tolerance—and for the freedom of others to define "civilization" for themselves—been heard two or three centuries earlier, this blot might not loom so large today.

In chapter 3 I mentioned as an aside that we may consider Boasian relativism as an improvement over the Victorian anthropologists' ideas about Western superiority. The Victorian view lent ideological support not only to the imposition of Western standards on others, but also to exploitation, for many believed that the savages would be better off under the political and economic tutelage of the more civilized nations. It was generally thought that we are in a better position than they to plan for their future and to make important decisions affecting them. The Boasian theory of relativism was a step forward because of the principle of tolerance and freedom it contained.

Pursuing this line of reasoning, a logical response of the Boasians to the criticism that their relativism is not value-free would be for them to concede. They could even turn the criticism to advantage as an additional justification for their relativity: surely the call for tolerance is a strength, not a weakness, of their moral philosophy.

To develop a moral theory around the principle of tolerance raises the need to justify that principle: what reasons or grounds can be given to make the case that cultural differences ought to be respected? The argument that seems to have been paramount to the Boasians was what I will call the empirical justification, or what Schmidt (1955) and others have called the *fact* of ethical relativism. According to this argument, the ethical principle (or theory) of tolerance follows from the empirical fact that cultures have different values. Given the evidence that there is no moral common denominator that all people share, it follows that the values of all societies deserve equal respect; certainly we cannot give our values preeminence over others. Herskovits in particular argued this position. He wrote:

> It is difficult to conceive of a systematic theory of cultural relativism . . . without the preexistence of the massive ethnographic documentation gathered by anthropologists concerning the similarities and differences between cultures the world over. Out of these data came the philosophical position [according to which there are no ethical universals or absolutes], and with the philosophical position came speculation as to its implications for conduct [which is that we ought to be tolerant of the other ways of life we encounter]. (1951, in 1973:39; cf. 1956, in 1973:90–94)

Philosophers have given two reasons why the argument about the factual variability of values is not a sufficient justification for tolerance. First, the evidence is open to dispute: anthropologists simply have not established that a pattern of radical variability exists within the sphere of moral beliefs. The differences in values that are cited—for example, the differences in views regarding parricide, whereby some societies feel it is right for children to put their parents to death, while others feel that such a practice is deplorable—may reflect differences in existential belief rather than morals. Earlier I distinguished between judgments of reality, or judgments about how the world is in fact—existential judgments—and judgments of value, or of how the world ought to be. Judgments of value are always made against a background of existential or factual beliefs and assumptions, consequently what appears to be a radical difference in values between societies may actually reflect different judgments of reality. Adapting an example used by William Frankena (1973:109–10; see also Duncker 1939), let us say that a society which has the custom of putting parents to death at an early age reasons in doing so that people are better off in the afterlife if they enter it while still physically vigorous. Both they and we presumably agree on the moral principle of looking out for our parents' interests, and our disagreement is really over the nature of the afterlife, and hence about what their interests are. This is a matter of factual belief, not values. If these people could convince us about the factual truth of their views about life after death, perhaps we would adopt their custom of dispatching our parents at an early age. Of course it may be that we would not believe it is right to kill our parents under any circumstances, in which case our difference with them is truly a fundamental one of moral judgment.

For the anthropologists to establish the claim about the radical differences in values among the world's populations, they would have to eliminate these differences in factual belief and compare pure moral values uncontaminated by existential ideas. Not only has this never been done, it would be most difficult, perhaps impossible.

A second reason why the argument about the variability of values cannot justify the ethical relativists' call for tolerance is that the factual evidence is beside the point. The relativists make the error of deriving an "ought" statement from an "is" statement (Schmidt 1955:783–84). To say that values vary from culture to culture is to describe (accurately or not) an empirical state of affairs in the real world, whereas the call for tolerance is a value judgment of what ought to be, and it is logically impossible to derive the one from the other. The fact of moral diversity no more compels our approval of other ways of life than the existence of cancer compels us to value ill-health.

Let us assume that we do find a set of values shared by all cultures. Would the relativist want to claim that these moral principles are legitimate ones for the world to embrace? What if the universal standard we discover is that all people are intolerant of other cultures—which is not very far-fetched? Clearly the ethical relativists would not throw aside their value of tolerance, but they would be forced to recognize that it is an error to think that the presence or absence of universal values among human cultures is a suitable base on which to build a moral philosophy.

How should we arrive at valid moral principles if not by examining the anthropological evidence? How can we go about justifying the call for tolerance? By rational argument, critical thought, the logical analysis of moral ideas. Herskovits believed that anthropologists' findings about the variability of values took the question of moral theory from the philosopher and gave it to the anthropologist, yet he was wrong. This is not to say that anthropologists should not join the discussion, but they should understand the ground rules in doing so: they enter the sphere of ethics in philosophy, and this has both a long history and an imposing literature. Nor is this to say that anthropologists' empirical findings are totally irrelevant. For instance, cases from foreign societies may pose moral questions the solution to which will help us clarify our moral ideas, the way legal cases help formulate law in areas in which it is unclear. But anthropologists' findings in these instances will serve as a basis for critical analysis and not empirical generalization.

In addition to the empirical justification, the Boasians sometimes used another rationale for their moral theory of tolerance, which was to suggest that other values are "equally valid," "fitting," or "appropriate" (for instance, Herskovits 1947:76; Benedict 1934a:278). How then do we assess the appropriateness of an institution? On what grounds do we judge that it is valid or fitting? On esthetic grounds? Practical ones?

Benedict and Herskovits were surprisingly vague on this point, although they tended to vacillate between two principles for assessing fitness. One was cultural consistency: a cultural feature is fitting if it is consistent with the rest of the cultural milieu. For instance, values which place substantial moral obligations on kinsmen (such as obligations of mutual aid and defense) are appropriate in a society that is organized on the basis of kinship. The criterion of cultural consistency reflected the Boasian view about the tendency for cultures to become integrated around a set of dominant values, as well as the Boasian tendency to value cultures that are coherent wholes. Yet this is a very unsatisfactory principle for judging the validity of institutions. By this criterion, presumably, torture is appropriate in a society which emphasizes violence, and intolerance is fitting among a people who value conformity.

A second criterion that sometimes appeared in Herskovits' and Benedict's work was the practical one, according to which an institution is appropriate because it has a certain practical value. For instance, the Dahomey practiced polygyny, a custom which strikes many Americans as barbaric in its requirement that a woman share her husband's affections with one or more co-wives in the family compound. Yet on closer analysis it emerges that Dahomean polygyny has several points in its favor. One is that the polygynous household has an economic stability that the nonpolygynous household lacks, for several wives form a considerable work force. A woman with co-wives does not have to work as hard as a woman without. Another advantage is that a woman is able to space her children better in a polygynous household, for co-wives make it feasible for her to avoid sexual relations with her husband for a period of time after having a child (Herskovits 1947:61–63).

The practical criterion has a very strong appeal, yet it also raises problems for Boasian thought. To the Boasians, each culture is the result of the processes of diffusion and integration, and these are virtually arbitrary relative to the practical needs or conveniences of the members of society (see Hatch 1973a:72–73, 86–89). It is sheer chance when an institution happens to have material benefits. Benedict (1934a:34–35) remarked upon the tendency for cultural traits to become inconvenient and cumbersome, to develop in ways that run di-

rectly counter to practical interests. For instance, the Kurnai of Australia had a custom whereby a young man had to choose his wife from
among the women of the local group, yet it was frequently the case
that there were no marriageable females in the locality. All the women
were either married already, or were related to the prospective groom
and thus ineligible according to a complex system of exogamous rules.
Even in the face of such difficulties, however, practical necessity did
not induce a change in the highly impractical cultural system. Kurnai
custom left the young couple with no choice but to elope—and to be
killed if caught in time, or to be given a severe beating upon return if
they were able both to escape and to remain away long enough to
have a child. Benedict wrote that "The Kurnai meet their cultural
dilemma typically enough. They have extended and complicated a
particular aspect of behaviour until it is a social liability."

The practical criterion for assessing the validity of institutions seems
quite inappropriate for such Boasians as Herskovits and Benedict because to them practical considerations simply do not play a large role
in the development of cultures and would apply to relatively few cultural features. Yet this measure of validity is too important to dismiss,
for it has considerable appeal today in supporting the call for tolerance. To find a suitable theoretical basis for it we need to step outside
Boasian thought and look at a different intellectual tradition in anthropology. This is the tradition of functionalism, which has its home
primarily in Britain, and is especially prominent in the work of the
British anthropologists Bronislaw Malinowski and A. R. Radcliffe-
Brown (see Hatch 1973a:214–335). In turning to functionalism we
also come to the second version of ethical relativism that I mentioned
above, which is the functionalist version.

The key element of functional theory in anthropology is that institutions have effects, or functions, that normally are beneficial to the
members of society. For instance, Radcliffe-Brown posited that the
function of religion is to promote social solidarity and cohesion by
sacralizing key elements of the social structure. His analysis of ances-
tor worship is illustrative. The principle of patrilineal descent is crucial
in a society that is organized into patrilineal lineages, for the entire
social structure is framed on this rule of descent. Political rights and

duties, economic organization, and legal relations of all kinds are defined according to patrilineality—lineage-mates are not only kinsmen, but have joint rights over property, are obligated to defend one another in the feud, and so on. It is essential for the principle of patrilineality to be reinforced, for should it weaken, and should the people no longer order themselves into patrilineages, the society would disintegrate into chaos. Religious ritual in which the patrilineal ancestors are worshiped serves to sacralize the rule of patrilineality and hence to reinforce the social structure.

Notice that the function of an institution is not usually obvious. The members of society generally do not grasp the beneficial effects which their institutions have, and the anthropologist must dig very deeply to find them. To the functionalists this helps explain why anthropologists like Benedict were so wrong in thinking that cultures develop almost randomly with respect to practical considerations: the practical effects of institutions were not carefully searched for, consequently they eluded the Boasians when they undertook field research. Radcliffe-Brown and Malinowski believed as most functionalists do today that there is very little that is useless in culture. Even a seemingly insignificant myth may reinforce some important part of society, while magical beliefs may help alleviate anxiety and enable people to cope in difficult circumstances, and warfare may help solidify the organization of those who join in battle against a common enemy.

The functionalist version of ethical relativism has it that although such foreign practices as bride-price, blood feud, and painful initiation rites may strike us as morally wrong, our disapproval is misplaced, for customs like these generally are vindicated by their useful effects. If we were to put a stop to the blood feud, for example, we may cause some unexpected problems in the society in which it occurs. Put somewhat differently, institutions are the way they are for good reason, and to interfere with them is to meddle with the natural order of things.

Functionalism has strong appeal in part because it is empirical. If colonial administrators or missionaries set out to eradicate cultural beliefs or practices on grounds that they are immoral or harmful, the anthropologist may counter by showing that the traits in question serve important functions and that we should not interfere with them.

The functionalist version of ethical relativism has a main feature that sets it apart from the Boasian version. This is that the idea of social function contains a criterion that can be used as a general or cross-cultural standard for evaluating institutions: the religious patterns of a foreign society can be judged by their beneficial effects, and so can the custom of bridewealth in another society, and the blood feud in still a third, and so on. Functionalists do not agree on the precise form of this universal value; in other words, they do not fully agree on what the benefits are that institutions serve, or the ends toward which they are directed. Radcliffe-Brown was fairly consistent in stressing social stability and cohesion; to him this is the end toward which institutions are oriented by and large, and it is a benign end, for it is better to live in a stable and cohesive society than a chaotic one. On the other hand, Malinowski often (but not always) employed an anxiety-reduction scheme. For instance, according to him, magic has the effect of reducing anxieties. So do beliefs in an afterlife, which make the prospect of death less traumatic. Malinowski assumed that people benefit somehow by having their anxieties reduced—presumably they are better able to cope as a result.

Here then is justification for tolerance. By contrast, Boasian ethical relativism takes a skeptical attitude toward this evaluative criterion. According to Boasian theory, the practical value that the functionalists believe they have identified is not a universal at all, for cultures differ in the importance they place on practical considerations. In other words, cultures vary according to the vicissitudes of history even with regard to this seemingly crucial feature. For example, the Pueblo Indians value social cohesiveness, whereas the Kwakiutl do not (see Hatch 1973a:237–38), just as some people value material comfort and others do not.

As a form of relativism functionalism has problems, one of which is that the value it harbors, the criterion by which it establishes that an institution is beneficial and therefore good, leads to some very questionable value judgments. Radcliffe-Brown's theory is illustrative. His approach was based on an analogy between society and biological organisms, in that just as a living creature has a physical structure, physiological needs, and organs which contribute to its overall health and persistence, so do human social systems. For example, there are defense mechanisms in the body which function to attack foreign elements that enter the blood stream, just as in society the religious system functions to stimulate moral sentiments in people's minds and thereby to contain selfish drives and interpersonal conflict that could damage the social order. Radcliffe-Brown sometimes referred to the "health" of a social system, using that term in a way very similar to its meaning in biology or medicine. Biological organisms, he wrote, will literally die if they are unable adequately to defend themselves when attacked by disease. Societies do not expire in this sense, but are "thrown into a condition of functional disunity or inconsistency." Like an organism struggling against disease, the society will "struggle toward some sort of eunomia, some kind of social health" (1935, in 1952:182–83).

In medicine the criterion of health is reasonably uncomplicated and straightforward, or at least it is if we deal strictly with physical as opposed to emotional and psychosomatic maladies. Health here is almost too obvious to need definition. Who would accuse a patient of malingering who appeared at the doctor's office dragging a broken leg or spitting blood? What physician would not register concern about a patient with a temperature of 104°, a low blood count, or evidence of cancer? On the other hand, what would the physician's reaction be to a patient who complained of double-jointedness, large feet, or an advanced case of balding?

On the surface it might seem that Radcliffe-Brown's functional criterion of health is as clear-cut as the one in medicine—who could argue that the breakdown of social order, the spread of violence and extortion, are desirable? Yet should we choose stability at any cost? Is a society healthy because it is perfectly stable when it is run by a totalitarian regime that leaves no significant power in the hands of the people? There are other goods besides that of social order, one of which is personal freedom.

A classic paper on social stratification (Davis and Moore 1945) illustrates the moral problems to which functionalism leads. This paper argues that stratification is functionally necessary in apportioning inherently unequal responsibilities and rewards. Specifically, functionally important positions in society, such as the office of U.S. Senator or Chairman of the Board of United States Steel, are rewarded with high prestige, considerable material comforts, and so on. These rewards have the effect of motivating people to fill the positions and to perform the duties. Yet it has also been argued (Tumin 1953; Wrong 1959) that, assuming this functional analysis is correct, there is another side to the coin. Stratification stimulates both an intolerant, self-righteous elitism among the chosen few, and an alienated proletariat. Stratification also gives the elite classes the power to maintain the status quo, and hence it is a conservative influence even in situations in which change may be desirable.

The cultural materialist version of functionalism contends that Radcliffe-Brown was off the mark in his view of the beneficial effects of institutions. The prime representative of cultural materialism is Marvin Harris (see Harris 1968, 1974, 1977), to whom the point of an institution is not its role in contributing to social stability and cohesion, but in adapting society to the physical environment. Harris takes ecological adaptation, not the healthy organism, as his model. For example, he argues that warfare in primitive societies is a mechanism that keeps the population from blundering beyond the carrying capacity of the land (1974:61–80, 1977:33–54). First, primitive groups that engage heavily in warfare must abandon their gardens from time to time and seek new land because of the pressures of conflict. This has the result of placing prime land in fallow every few years and forcing the cultivation of formerly unused areas. The soil is thus less likely to be exhausted and a disastrous drop in the food supply is prevented. Second, intense warfare places a premium on males, who do most of the fighting. Consequently, female infanticide typically is a by-product of warfare—female infants frequently are either killed overtly at birth, or are allowed to die from neglect. Harris writes: "The study of primitive war leads to the conclusion that war has been part of an adaptive strategy associated with particular technological, demographic, and ecological conditions" (1974:79–80). He implies that warfare occurs when and where human societies stand to lose more from its absence than its presence—primitive peoples who engage in warfare are better off with than without it.*

Yet the benefits of warfare come at a very high cost. The Yanomamö of South America, cited by Harris as a case in which belligerence is ecologically adaptive, are illustrative. It is estimated that 7 percent of Yanomanö women die in battle, and that 33 percent of the adult men do so (Harris 1974:69). What is more, a very large percentage of the population is injured though not killed in combat, and a substantial number of children are killed through infanticide. These statistics give us pause—surely the Yanomanö could endure substantial ecological maladaptation before the level of human suffering would equal that which comes from the supposedly adaptive system of violence. Primitive warfare is, at least, a very roundabout and inefficient means for achieving the beneficial results that Harris' theory gives it. So we come to the same difficulty associated with the functionalism of Radcliffe-Brown: the standard that we are to use in judging the value of institutions may create as many moral problems as it solves.

Functionalism leads to a serious moral dilemma, but there is another problem as well in using functional theory as a basis for justifying tolerance. Some very serious objections have been raised against it as a theory of society. One objection concerns the functionalist claim that the unintended effects of institutions are usually or nearly always beneficial. Why are they not just as often neutral or even harmful? Or why are they not random relative to some general standard of beneficence or harmfulness? For instance, Malinowski's theory of magic held that magical ritual reduces anxiety by providing a form of substitute activity or displacement when a person is faced with uncertainty on a matter of importance. The fisherman goes to sea hoping both for a large catch and a safe return, and no amount of technical knowledge or practical experience will enable him to foretell what will happen. The anxiety builds, but it is relieved by the performance of a ritual.

Malinowski's theory could conceivably have stopped at that point;

* I infer this from Harris' statement that "we have every reason to hope that when humanity stands to lose more than it can possibly gain from war, other means of resolving intergroup conflicts will take its place" (1974:80).

he was not compelled by logic or evidence to add that, by reducing anxiety, magic enables the individual better to cope. Indeed, he could have argued the reverse with equal plausibility: it could be that the supposed tension reduction helps reduce the individual's attention to the problem at hand and thus to reduce his or her chances of dealing with it adequately. It is tempting to suggest that the functionalist tendency to see beneficial effects behind institutions is a manifestation of the view that nature is benign. Just as Herbert Spencer believed that the geological evolution of the earth has amounted to the progressive betterment of our planet, so the functionalists seem to suggest that behind all (or nearly all) the seemingly bizarre institutions of mankind there is something good to be found. The functionalists may be right, of course, but surely the general beneficence of institutions cannot be taken as a general rule without offering some very sound reasons to support it.

The functionalists actually do have a supporting argument, which is the claim (often made only implicitly) that institutions are a response to "needs" or exigencies. Radcliffe-Brown's theory of taboos is illustrative. According to him, the occurrence of taboos is not random or accidental; they exist for specific reasons, and hence occur where and when there is a need for them. Among the Andaman Islanders there are certain taboos associated with childbirth, including a prohibition on calling the mother and father by name, and an injunction against the parents' eating certain foods. It is no accident that these taboos are associated with parents and not someone else, and that they occur when the woman is about to have a child and not at some other point in time, for the taboos serve a specific function. They provide an "obligatory recognition in standardized symbolic form of the significance and importance of the event [of childbirth] to the parents and to the community at large" (1939, in 1952:150–51). The birth of a child is an important event indeed, for it constitutes the entry of a new member into society. Not only must someone assume the obligation of caring for the infant, but rights and duties of all kinds attach to the relatives of the child. The father, say, can eventually claim certain services from the child, and is legally responsible for damages the child may some day incur. The taboos which apply to the mother and father are analogous to a birth certificate, for they are a means for establishing citizenship, rights of inheritance, paternity, and so forth. The Andamanese taboos establish, and force the public recognition of, the legal status of an infant and of the mother and father (as well as their kinsmen) in relation to the infant. Rites of this kind "exist and persist because they are part of the mechanism by which an orderly society maintains itself in existence"; these functions constitute "the ultimate reason for [the] existence" of the rituals (p. 152).

Marvin Harris illustrates the functionalist claim that institutions are responses to basic exigencies. Harris chides anthropologists like Benedict for failing to explain custom. Too often, he maintains, differences in human life styles are described in the anthropological literature as insoluble puzzles. The anthropologist seems to imply that "only God knows why the Kwakiutl burn their houses. Ditto for why the Hindus refrain from eating beef, or the Jews and Moslems abhor pork, or why some people believe in messiahs while others believe in witches" (1974:3–4). Harris argues that materialist explanations are available to solve these seemingly inscrutable riddles: customs of even the most bizarre nature are responses to ecological exigencies. Warfare is an example. Or take the seemingly irrational belief among Jews and Moslems that the pig is an unclean animal that pollutes whoever tastes or touches it (pp. 35–45). Harris argues that the condemnation of the pig makes good sense given the "cultural and natural ecosystem of the Middle East" (p. 40). The pig is best adapted to forests and shaded river banks rather than the arid lands of the Old Testament and the Koran, and the food it eats makes it a competitor with human beings— it does not subsist on grass, as cattle do. The pig is not a practical source of milk, and it is difficult to herd. It is rather a luxury food, "esteemed for its succulent, tender, and fatty qualities" (p. 44). It is ecologically maladaptive in the Middle East, and "small-scale production would only increase the temptation" (p. 44). By placing a taboo on pig meat it was possible to concentrate on goats, sheep, and cattle, which are far more suitable to the environment. This Jewish and Islamic taboo is not a happenstance, but occurs under definite ecological conditions.

In reading Harris it is difficult to avoid the conclusion that virtually every custom is explainable by reference to a functional cause of some kind. As soon as he finishes "explaining one previously inscrutable custom or life style" he moves to another, which like the first has its solution in ecological principles (pp. v–vi). Radcliffe-Brown exhibited a similar tendency; he wrote that "in the life of a given community each element of the culture plays a specific part, has a specific function" (1929, in 1958:40).*

The question, now, is why the appropriate institution should occur when and where it is called for, and in the appropriate form? What is the principle, force, or mechanism that guides the proper development of institutions so that they have the beneficial and unintended effects that are claimed for them? Radcliffe-Brown engaged in sleight-of-hand when he dealt with this issue, for he denied that his functionalism was concerned with how institutions came to be (1941, in 1952:86). He wrote that he was interested in understanding the functions of institutions—how social systems work at the present time—and not how they developed. Yet he was also clear that institutions do not occur in random fashion, for certain usages appear in appropriate form when they are needed. So although he denied using the notion of cause in his analysis, he used it anyway.

Harris on the other hand explicitly offers a mechanism to explain the development of appropriate institutions. This is a form of natural selection which applies not to biological but to cultural traits (Harris 1960, 1971:150–62). According to Harris, the people who adhere to an adaptive trait tend better to survive than those who adhere to a maladaptive one, hence the superior trait is selected for through time. This mechanism appears in his discussion of the Hindu belief in the sacred cow. It may appear that the Hindu ideas about the sacredness of cattle, according to which the animals should not be slaughtered and eaten, are maladaptive, in that the cultural beliefs forestall the consumption of a plentiful foodstuff in India. But the trait is ecologically adaptive in a number of ways. For example, traction animals are indispensable in Indian agriculture, and if the oxen were slaughtered

---

* In the mid-1930s Radcliffe-Brown softened his insistence that every feature of culture has functional contributions; his later view was that they *may* have. See Hatch 1973a:219 n.2.

in times of crisis the next year's crop would never come to harvest (Harris 1974:11–32). The Hindu beliefs protect against potentially disastrous responses to short-term needs. How then did such a useful cultural trait become established? "The taboo on slaughter and beef eating," Harris writes, "may be as much a product of natural selection as the small bodies and fantastic recuperative powers of the zebu breeds" (p. 21). Farmers who killed their animals during drought or famine sealed their own doom; on the other hand, the survivors of a given crisis were those who held tenaciously to the belief. Their survival ensured the vitality of the belief. Again, Harris suggests that societies which "invented or adopted growth cutoff institutions," such as warfare, "survived more consistently than those that blundered forward across the limit of carrying capacity" (p. 66). Hence warfare proliferates where it is advantageous.

Here then is a principle which explains the adaptive tendency of institutions. Beneficial effects are selected for by a process that the members of society do not perceive, just as a population of parameciums need not understand the process of selection that is affecting them. Natural forces are constantly at work trimming and molding culture.

The mechanism of selection has some serious difficulties when it is applied to cultural phenomena, however. In biology, natural selection acts on the genes, or more accurately on the frequency of genes in a given population. If a trait such as protective coloration is adaptive, the individuals who carry the genes for this trait will have a slight edge and will live to produce a larger number of offspring than those without, hence the number of carriers of these genes will increase with each generation. There are a few other factors besides natural selection that can change gene frequencies, such as mutation and random drift, but these play a very insignificant role overall. By contrast, there is a multitude of factors that can conceivably affect the course of culture history. For instance, belief systems have internal logic, and culture change may consist of the progressive development of this logic. Again, a people may acquire a custom from neighbors simply because they hold their neighbors in high regard. To the extent that these other principles are at work, the importance of selective pressure is reduced.

In fact, it is perfectly consistent with all we know about culture at present to suggest that selection as Harris conceives it plays no role whatever in culture change. He may be right that it does, but at the moment, at least, neither the data nor reason forces the critic to concede.

It would seem that anthropology should respond to this disagreement by putting the question to the empirical test. Someone ought to do some careful field studies to see if Radcliffe-Brown was right about the function of religion, say, or Harris about the function of the Hindu belief in the sacredness of cattle. The question is not so easily resolved, however, and dozens of fieldworkers have worked on it. The difficulty is that social phenomena are enormously complicated—so far, at least, it has not been possible adequately to isolate all the factors involved in any functional hypothesis. For instance, the definitive test of Radcliffe-Brown's theory of ritual would be to remove the religious system entirely from a society in which religion plays a major role, and then watch to see if the social structure collapses. Of course no anthropologist has tried this, although something of the sort has occasionally been accomplished by colonial governments when they have suppressed indigenous religious practices. Any number of complications arise that make these historical cases hard to evaluate, however. Where native religions have genuinely been destroyed, as among the Plains Indians, the spread of Western civilization has also undermined the native economic system, traditional patterns of authority, and so on, any one of which could account for the disintegration of the social structure. Virtually all specific functional hypotheses remain plausible but untested propositions.*

To summarize, there have been two somewhat different versions of ethical relativism in anthropology. The first is the Boasian, which claims to be value free in assessing foreign peoples, although its central feature is a value judgment about the intrinsic worth of other cultures. It proposes a theory of value according to which we should respect other ways of life. Behind this value in turn is the basic moral

---

* Harris' most concerted effort to establish a particular functional hypothesis is his work on the sacred cow of India. See Harris 1974:11–34, 269; 1977:141–52.

belief that people ought to be free to live as they choose. This set of ideals seems reasonable enough, yet Boasian thought does not provide suitable grounds to justify the assertion about the intrinsic worth of other cultures. We are left without a response to the question *why* we should be tolerant, hence we face the dilemma of having a potentially worthy moral theory but no good reason for adhering to it.

The second version of relativism is the functionalist, which is like the Boasian in urging tolerance, but which provides a more explicit rationale in doing so. It holds that institutions normally exist for good reason, in that they have unintended and beneficial effects. Yet the functionalist version of ethical relativism has its own problems, for it leads to some unhappy dilemmas concerning the evaluation of institutions—it leads to the approval of practices that are patently inhumane. Besides, as a theory of culture or society it is open to dispute. In particular, the functionalists do not provide convincing reasons to support the claim that institutions normally have beneficial effects, and the empirical evidence is too equivocal to offer much help. So we come to the same conclusion here as in the case of Boasian ethical relativism, which is that the anthropologists have not supplied a satisfactory justification for the moral theory of tolerance. They cannot give an adequate answer to the skeptic who asks why tolerance is a more reasonable principle to guide us in our relations with foreign peoples than any other principle. This is a major issue, for the call for tolerance is at the core of ethical relativism—it is the primary reason why relativism has such strong appeal.

FURTHER READING

The philosophical literature on relativism is substantial. For journal articles, consult *The Philosopher's Index* (see the entries "cultural relativism," "ethical relativism," and "relativism"). Good summary articles are found in *The Encyclopedia of Philosophy* (Brandt 1967) and the *International Encyclopedia of the Social Sciences* (Bidney 1968; Emmet 1968). A variety of books deal with relativism, and I found two in particular to be useful: Brandt's *Ethical Theory* (1959: chs. 5 and 11), and Moser's *Absolutism and Relativism in Ethics* (1968). Other useful books are Brandt 1954; Edel 1955; Edel and Edel 1959; Ladd 1957; MacBeath 1952; Phillips and Mounce 1970: ch. 7; Rudolph 1968; and Stace 1962: chs. 1 and 2. During the 1970s several philosophers began to express less negative views about ethical relativism than before and to suggest that the case against it might not be as certain as generally believed. See Philippa Foot, *Moral Relativism* (1978).

A useful discussion of the factual variability of values is contained in Brandt 1959:92–103. His tentative conclusion is that there are radical differences in values among societies. On the other hand, a number of anthropologists have suggested that the earlier claim about the radical differences in values may be mistaken; see Kluckhohn 1953, 1955; Linton 1954; Redfield 1957.

Functionalists have not often written explicitly about relativism, although it is a more or less implicit theme in much of their work. For Malinowski, see especially *Magic, Science, and Religion and Other Essays* (1948), and for Radcliffe-Brown see *Method in Social Anthropology* (1958) and *Structure and Function in Primitive Society* (1952). A work by a philosopher who is strongly in support of the functionalist version of ethical relativism is MacBeath's *Experiments in Living* (1952).

A more critical view is taken by Moser (1968:105–20, 132–40). A large literature is devoted to analyzing functionalism as anthropological theory. See, among others, Beattie 1964:49–64; Erasmus 1967; Jarvie 1973:17–36.

CHAPTER FIVE

The Limits of Tolerance

THE anthropologists' theory of ethical relativism is clearly wanting, because the case for tolerance has not been made. On the other hand, this is not a good reason to reject it outright, because the case may still be makable. Anthropologists are not philosophers, after all, and they simply may be slow to work out the philosophical underpinnings of a theory that is quite worthy.

In this chapter I take a somewhat different tack from the last. Having suggested that the case for tolerance has not been made, I now suggest that it cannot be made, or at least not without revising the original notion of relativism in some major fashion. The main thrust of this chapter is that, in its call for tolerance, ethical relativism goes too far by giving indiscriminate approval to every foreign institution.

The functionalist version of ethical relativism is not guilty of this in principle, for presumably it supplies a standard for distinguishing between institutions which are harmful (or dysfunctional) and beneficial. But given the difficulty of testing hypotheses about the usefulness and harmfulness of institutions, functionalist anthropologists almost always stress or "discover" beneficial effects.* The mere fact of a society's existence is often taken as evidence that it is "a functioning harmonious whole," the parts of which are essential (Gregg and Williams 1948:600). As a result, the critics of functionalism often take it to task for fostering a conservative attitude toward change.†

---

* Certainly this is true when they consider primitive societies, and less so when they turn to complex Western civilizations, for they often turn cynical and critical as they focus on their own culture. I will discuss Leslie White from this point of view in chapter 6.

† Stanislav Andreski offers one of the most virulent attacks on the conservatism of functionalism (Andreski 1972:144–54).

The Boasian version of ethical relativism is subject to even harsher criticism than the functionalist in its commitment to the status quo. The approval it enjoins seems to be absolute, leaving no room for judgment. For instance, Herskovits commented:

> cultural relativism is a philosophy which, in recognizing the values set up by every society to guide its own life, lays stress on the dignity inherent in every body of custom, and on the need for tolerance of conventions though they may differ from one's own. . . . [T]he relativistic point of view brings into relief the validity of every set of norms for the people whose lives are guided by them, and the values these represent. (1947:76)

Presumably there is no justification for any judgment but approval.

A person does not have to dig very deeply into the literature to see the moral dilemma this creates. An example comes from the work of an Australian anthropologist, Ian Hogbin. He was a lieutenant colonel in the Australian army during World War II, and was assigned to gather information on natives involved in the conflict. In 1944 he was asked to report on a small New Guinea village that seemed to be particularly ill-disposed, perhaps even disloyal, to the Australian government. The village, Busama, was located on the coast of New Guinea in an area of considerable military activity. The region was under Australian control when the war started, but was overrun by the Japanese in 1942, and retaken by the Australians who then set up a military base a few miles from Busama. The village had been severely bombed—every hut and canoe was destroyed, along with domestic goods, gardens, and virtually everything else. When the Australians recaptured the area the war was at its height and the armed forces desperately needed manpower. The people of Busama were ordered to make thatch for the base that was going up, and in return the natives were given provisions and the promise of cash payment. The able-bodied men were conscripted to help in construction and other heavy tasks in the region.

Hogbin discovered that it was more than the military campaign that was besetting the village; it seems the native headman was causing nearly as much harm as the war.

The village headmen in Australian New Guinea were chosen from among the local native leaders to serve as liaison with the territorial administration. In theory, the white district officer merely chose the chief of each village to serve as headman, or luluai. Village structure was not as clear-cut as the administration thought, however, and each locale had a number of influential men who were more or less in competition for prestige. By appointing an official luluai, the administration elevated one of several local influentials to a central position of authority, for that person was supported by the full power of the administration, and the traditional system of leadership soon deteriorated. It was not usually the best people, nor even the most popular influentials, who were selected as headmen, partly because it was difficult or impossible for the district officer to know enough about each locale to make the wisest choice.

The headman in Busama was a man named Bumbu. He had held office since 1926, save that he fled when the Japanese captured the area and was eventually caught and imprisoned by them. But after the Australians returned he was reappointed as luluai. The story Hogbin uncovered was the following:

Bumbu had a terrible reputation from the start. He was often brutal to village members, caning them unmercifully when displeased. On one occasion he struck a woman on the face, permanently blinding her, so that she had to be led about by a small child. Bumbu seduced two young women, one of whom bore a bastard; the other was his niece, hence the relationship was incestuous and morally reprehensible to the people. Both women were too terrified of Bumbu to admit to authorities that he was responsible. The villagers complained of these and other grievances to a succession of district officers, but Bumbu denied the charges, convincing the authorities that the complaints were malicious attacks by those who bore grudges against him. Perhaps it was also easier for the district officers to ignore the complaints than to act on them. Whatever the reason, nothing was done and the villagers became resigned to the oppression that Bumbu imposed. For instance, on one occasion he demanded that the villagers contribute to the purchase of a boat which he then used as a charter craft for Europeans, keeping the profit for himself. If local people needed to use the boat, they had to pay even higher rates than the Europeans. The people had no choice but to submit.

Bumbu fled when the Japanese occupied the region because he feared reprisal from the villagers now that his source of authority had disappeared. When the Australians recaptured the area, he fabricated a story about his heroism—he supposedly refused to denounce Australia when the Japanese demanded he do so and was both imprisoned and tortured as a result. In addition, he told the Australian authorities that the villagers had willingly aided the enemy and tried to bring about their victory. Bumbu manufactured circumstantial evidence to support his case, and was convincing; he was awarded the Loyal Service medal, whereas the village gained a reputation for disloyalty to Australia.

When he was reinstalled as headman, Bumbu set out in vengeance to humiliate and starve the people. When rations came he took far more than his share, selling what he did not need. He kept the people from raising food by forcing them to dance during the afternoons and evenings when they should have been in the gardens. Those who were late to the dances were forced to sit for several hours with their hands in the latrine, and dancers who did not do their best, and spectators who fell asleep, were given the stick. While he and his small band of supporters were idle, the others were forced to make the thatch that had been ordered by the army; the villagers also collected firewood for him and his associates, and built him a new house—whereas they lived in make-shift huts created after their own' houses had been destroyed by bombs. Bumbu had six elaborately dressed young women, kinswomen, as part of his retinue; he offered them to troops as prostitutes, presumably against their will, and had sexual relations with at least two of them himself.

Once Hogbin discovered the truth about Bumbu he presented his evidence to the district officer, who called a public inquiry and had the headman removed (Hogbin 1951:chs. 1, 8).

It is true that the Australian administration in New Guinea must take much of the blame for Bumbu's oppression, for they conferred authority on him and failed to act when there were clear signs that something was amiss. Still, he was not their puppet; he was not duped or corrupted by them, nor was he carrying out their policy. He was a shrewd, ambitious, vindictive man, and he consciously deceived and manipulated the district officers.

The relativists may argue that their theory does not lead them to approve Bumbu's actions because he went *against* custom; he can be judged by the values of his own society and not ours. Pursuing this line of reasoning, imagine that one of the major elements of this case were altered. Let us say that the Australian administration did not enter into the picture at all as the basis of his rule, and that instead the source of Bumbu's power was his control over traditional economic resources and the use of force. He was the same ambitious, vindictive person, humiliating and punishing his opponents with the same vengeance he exhibited in real life, and the majority of the villagers were as strongly opposed to him, yet they were powerless to act. Let us say further that Hogbin is to visit these people as an anthropologist. Would he be obligated to approve this state of affairs, as the relativist must argue, since it concerned the people of another culture? In the Busama of real life Hogbin intervened on the villagers' behalf, and surely he acted properly in doing so. Would it not be as reasonable for him to intervene under these imaginary circumstances?

A second case illustrates the dilemma we are led to by the ethical relativists' call for blanket approval of foreign practices. This is the pattern of violence among the Yanomamö, who have been studied by Napoleon Chagnon over a period of years starting in 1964. These people live in heavily fortified villages scattered through the dense, tropical rain forest of a remote region where the borders of Venezuela and Brazil meet. Violence is a constant theme in interpersonal relations at all levels among the Yanomamö. Warfare is chronic, stimulated largely by disputes over women and their abductions. Weaker groups are driven from their gardens by repeated attacks and are forced to find sanctuary among allies, who can never be trusted, for they may be planning a massacre of their own, killing the men and keeping the women; even the ally that offers a genuinely safe sanctuary can be expected to demand women in return for its help.

A series of incidents illustrates the Yanomamö pattern of violence. In about 1949 one Yanomamö village, the Upper Bisaasi-teri, decided to move to a new, remote location because of a prolonged war with its neighbors. Soon after moving, the villagers were invited to a feast with their new neighbors, only to be set upon by their hosts; some of the Upper Bisaasi-teri men were killed, others were badly wounded but escaped, and a number of the women were abducted; the survivors who escaped fled to their newly cleared garden, which was not yet productive but much safer than the village site. Eventually the head-man of still another village visited Upper Bisaasi-teri and invited the people to live with his group. The invitation was accepted, inasmuch as the Upper Bisaasi-teri now were too few in number either to defend themselves or to continue the war against their enemies. However, they knew that the newfound benefactors were not acting out of kind-ness, for they would demand a number of women in return for the alliance and protection. It happens that the hosts had something else afoot as well: when the opportunity came they would kill all the men of Upper Bisaasi-teri and appropriate the women. But fortunately for the guests, an unexpected outbreak of hostilities with still another vil-lage led the hosts to postpone the massacre. Before opportunity came for the hosts to carry out their plan, the Upper Bisaasi-teri moved to a new village site, and soon struck a deal with neighbors in their new locale. These neighbors were on relatively amicable terms with an-other village, which was an archenemy of the Upper Bisaasi-teri. The neighbor village would call a feast for the archenemies, and together with the Upper Bisaasi-teri would kill all the men and divide the women among themselves. It happens that many of the intended victims were ill at the time of the feast, so only five men and four women came; three of the men were killed and two escaped, whereas all the women were abducted (Chagnon 1977:76–79).

The unhappy plight of Yanomamö women is a theme running throughout these episodes, for they were given to allies by their kins-men in return for protection, and abducted by enemies. Their fate upon abduction illustrates the level of violence among these people.

A woman who is captured is raped by all the men in the raiding party, and later by the men in the village who were not on the raid. She then becomes the wife of one of the villagers (p. 123). The woman assumes difficult and laborious tasks as a wife, whether she is abducted by enemies or married into her own village. Women must be obedient to their husbands and wait upon them attentively, and they are frequently punished, sometimes brutally. They are occasionally beaten, shot with barbed arrows, chopped with machetes or axes, and burned with firebrands. Because a woman's brothers are her main protectors, she dreads being married through abduction or other means to a man in a distant village (pp. 81–83).

Children are subjected to violence. Infanticide is practiced if the mother is still nursing an older child, and the first-born is killed if it is a female. Sometimes a child is killed because the mother feels she cannot take care of it properly or because it would be an inconvenience to her. Chagnon describes one incident that he observed. A well-fed young mother was eating while her two-year-old child— "emaciated, filthy, and nearly starved"—kept reaching for a share. The mother explained that some time ago the child had gotten diarrhea and did not eat for several days, and as a result her milk dried up, yet the child was too young to know how to eat other foods. Chagnon insisted she give the baby food, which it ate ravenously. "In short, she was letting the baby die slowly of starvation" (pp. 74–75). Chagnon tells of another incident that happened several years before he arrived among the Yanomamö. A group of men raided an enemy village, killing the headman and several others, and abducted the headman's young son. The son was taken to live in the village of his captors, but was "persecuted and tormented" by the other children. One of the men "got sick of seeing this, so he shot the little boy as he was bathing in the stream" (p. 122).

Chagnon has described the violence of the Yanomamö quite vividly, and these people have become well known in the literature for their fierceness and brutality. On the other hand, Chagnon stresses that "the Yanomamö do not spend all or even a major fraction of their waking hours making war on neighbors or abusing their wives." What is more, warfare is intense at particular times, but almost stops at other times. Individuals in Yanomamö society also exhibit considerable warmth and affection toward one another, as well as humor and happiness. The pattern of violence is marked, but the tender emotions are evident as well (pp. 162–63).

A strict ethical relativist might argue that Bumbu's tyranny differed from the case of Yanomamö violence in that the former was an instance of an individual going against custom, whereas Yanomamö violence is an expression of the people's values, consequently we are justified in criticizing Bumbu but not the Yanomamö. This is a way of life that is proper for these people. For instance, Yanomamö women seem to value the damage their husbands inflict, for wives sometimes measure how much their husbands care for them by how often they are beaten (p. 83). Similarly, men value warfare inasmuch as it is prestigious to have the reputation of a fierce and courageous fighter. Yet this argument is mistaken. The women do not look forward to the beatings they receive, otherwise they would not prefer to marry someone from their own village for the protection this gives, nor would they flee in terror when their husbands come at them with a machete. What is more, the men are clearly fearful during warfare (e.g., see pp. 135–37), and they engage in raids chiefly out of a sense of duty and as a result of social pressure. Even if some of the Yanomamö genuinely do cherish the values of violence, others feel victimized; in their view, not just the outsider's, they are forced by others to accept injury and deprivation that they do not want. Bumbu's villagers wanted an end to his tyranny no less than the emaciated Yanomamö child wanted food, the wife wanted to avoid the arrow shot in her thigh, or the man wanted to sleep in his hammock and not have his head opened with an axe.

The moral principle of tolerance that is proposed by Boasian relativism carries the obligation that one cannot be indifferent toward other ways of life—it obligates us to approve what others do. So if missionaries or government officials were to interfere in Yanomamö affairs for the purpose of reducing violence, the relativist would be obligated to oppose these moves in word if not action. Similarly, by the strict logic of relativism, Chagnon was wrong to insist that the mother feed her emaciated child. The Boasian relativist is placed in the morally awkward position of endorsing the infant's starvation, the rape of abducted women, the massacre of whole villages. We are asked to approve as the child bathing in the stream is shot with an arrow. The functionalists are led to a similar conclusion: Harris contends that Yanomamö warfare and infanticide are ecologically adaptive in that they keep the population within the carrying capacity of the land. Approval is warranted on practical grounds, even though the practical value of the institutions is asserted but not proved.

A third case is an especially poignant illustration of the moral dilemma to which the relativists' call for tolerance leads us. This is the case of honor killings among the rural Arabs of the West Bank of the Jordan River. Among these people a woman's family and kin are morally dishonored if she bears a child out of wedlock, and the only way to restore the honor is to kill her—even if her pregnancy was due to rape, or if it came about because she led such a sheltered life that she did not understand the biology of sex. The man who is involved in such cases is not subject to serious retribution, for it is the woman who must pay—and she is usually no more than a teen-ager. Typically she flees for her life, or hides, but her male relatives usually catch her; she may even be tricked into returning home by being told she is forgiven. She is killed by poison, sometimes by being stabbed or burned to death. It seems that a small, secret group has formed to save these women: to give them abortions if they want, and to smuggle them away, usually to Europe, where they find jobs. This group consists of a network of Jews, Christians, and Arabs, and is financed by a European foundation and headquartered in Jerusalem. The members operate in secrecy to protect both the women and themselves—they too may be killed by the relatives for interfering with family honor.

According to the logic of relativism, this group of protectors is wrong, for it violates the moral beliefs of another people—moral beliefs which are not trifling, but which are held with great conviction and which are deeply rooted in the traditions of this part of the world. To spirit away these pregnant women is to force their kinsmen to suffer dishonor (Torgerson 1981).

The alternative to tolerance, which is to engage in or to endorse interference of some kind, is clearly a thicket, for virtually anything a person might do on behalf of those who feel victimized may carry a price—witness the dishonor suffered by the women's relatives in the case of honor killings cited above. To cite another instance, if one intervenes on behalf of the abducted Yanomamö woman, one will necessarily infringe on the freedom of the abductors. In their view they have a perfect right to rape her and to force her to become another man's wife in a foreign village. Yet several points can be made to clarify the problems surrounding interference of this kind. First is the rather obvious one that a price is to be paid if one does *not* interfere. This is what stimulates the charge that relativism is inherently conservative: in the face of a state of affairs that is unfair or inhumane, the relativist responds with the moral judgment of tolerance. Tolerance in this context is not a matter of neutrality at all, but a moral commitment to the status quo, whatever that may mean for the well-being of some.

Second, we need to separate two questions that are easily confused. On one hand is that of whether or not we should disapprove of the behavior or institution in question—that is, whether or not it is legitimate to make a negative value judgment in a given instance. On the other is the question of what we should do about it if we decide to disapprove. Disapproving an action or institution is quite a different matter from arriving at an appropriate response to our disapproval. For instance, one could agree with the Catholic missionaries living among the Yanomamö in their disapproval of certain Yanomamö practices, but disagree over what to do about them. The issue of establishing grounds for disapproving of other ways of life falls in the province of philosophy, whereas the issue of how to respond to a negative judgment once it is made falls in the province of social engineering. We may find ourselves completely stymied at the level of social engineering, and not have the slightest idea what we should do in response to the harm we see; yet this does not force us to approve what we find.

Third, it is not true that interference is inherently harmful, and Chagnon's insistence that the mother feed her emaciated child is a case in point. What possible objection could be raised to his action in this case? The Australian administration in New Guinea is, among other things, a form of institutionalized intervention which is logically analogous to Chagnon's act. In theory it ought to be possible to structure the administration in such a way that it operates with reasonable effectiveness and probity, and thus to establish living conditions that the native peoples would prefer over their indigenous way of life. In other words, the issue of social engineering may be a very tough one to solve, but there is no reason to believe it is inherently impossible to do so.

In mentioning the possibility of intervention in other cultures I do not mean to invoke the nineteenth-century notion that primitives need the guidance of a superior civilization. The image I have in mind rather is that of the passer-by who happens upon a crime of violence and stops to help the victim. It is true that the possibility always exists that something may go wrong—I may mistake victim for villain, for instance. But if we hear screams in a dark alley, how can we walk away and say it is none of our business? And should we stop to help, we do not signify that we believe we are superior to either the wrongdoer or the sufferer.

Setting aside the question of intervention and focusing on the matter of disapproval, we need to be clear about the grounds by which we may disapprove the actions and institutions of other societies. Expressed somewhat differently, at what point does our tolerance stop? What Bumbu's tyranny, Yanomamö violence, and honor killing on the West Bank of the Jordan River have in common that makes tolerance so difficult to defend is the use of unmistakable, unmitigated coercion—"the deliberate forceful interference in the affairs of human beings by other human beings" (Feinberg 1973:7). Stated in this fashion it is clear that what is at issue is freedom or, better, a particular kind of freedom—it is not freedom from frustration, say, or from hard work, but freedom from the deliberate coercion of others. Tolerance should not extend to actions and institutions in which coercion is used against human beings.*

Granted, it is not easy to use the principle of coercion in judging foreign institutions, for it entails a framework of concepts that are somewhat imprecise, including the notions of victimization (someone must feel harmed, injured, or threatened by someone else), force and the threat of force, and such individual affairs as security of life and property that someone else is able to interfere with. A crucial but especially difficult part of this framework is the distinction between legitimate and illegitimate coercion. Usually there is some form of authority in society whereby both the individual's and the public's interests are protected, and this authority is normally backed by force. This is legitimate coercion—it is hardly the same as the coercion of the rapist or extortionist—and does not warrant disapproval. Yet questions are constantly raised about the legitimacy of the policies of the legal authorities, such as whether a war that is being waged is a just one; and it often happens that not everyone in a society accepts the legitimacy of those who occupy office. The concepts of legitimacy and illegitimacy clearly are not simple ones to apply. Another difficulty is that people in other cultures perceive and interpret one another's actions in terms very different from our own, and it is necessary to "translate" their customs and actions into our frame of reference to make sense of them. This always raises the possibility of some distortion of meaning and misunderstanding of behavior. For instance, there are societies in which most private possessions are not truly one's own, for kinsmen and friends may be entitled to borrow them almost without restriction, and in some cases if an item is asked for it cannot properly be refused. If for good reason a person does refuse what is considered a normal request, is it coercion if the item is forcibly taken? An event like this needs to be clearly understood from the perspective

* For an analysis of the concepts of freedom, liberty, harm, and coercion, see Feinberg 1973:1–54. In chapter 7 I will have more to say about the philosophical status of this principle of coercion as it is used in this book. I will suggest that although it is not given full philosophical justification here, it is warranted on prima facie grounds.

of the people themselves before it can be evaluated according to the set of ideas I am suggesting here.

It may be very difficult to apply the criterion of coercion in specific cases, but it should still be possible to do so with at least fair success. After all, the courts face difficult decisions concerning damages, injury, and harm on a daily basis, and they have arrived at a very sophisticated set of principles for deciding them. The guidelines that are needed for judging across cultural boundaries are poorly developed, yet it seems reasonable that they could be sharpened if there were sufficient need.

The use of the principle of coercion does not nullify ethical relativism, for the two are properly seen as adjuncts to one another. Unless a foreign practice involves illegitimate coercion, it ought to receive approval—we are obligated to be morally tolerant of foreign practices short of coercion. And the justification for this tolerance is the value of freedom. People ought to be free to live as they choose. Take the case of polygyny. One reason why Western Europeans have disapproved of plural marriage in other societies is the moral belief that it is simply wrong for a man to be sexually intimate with more than one woman. By itself this is insufficient, for an adequate argument would have to suggest that polygyny does someone harm. Such an argument does sometimes occur, for some believe that polygyny is degrading to women by requiring them to share their affections for a man with one or more co-wives, all of whom are forced to live with jealousy and discontentment. This argument comes close to qualifying for a legitimate justification for disapproval, except for a serious flaw: it is factually wrong. With few exceptions, women in polygynous households are not coerced and do not feel victimized. The belief that they are is based on the mistake of viewing a foreign institution in terms of our own cultural perspective. In this case we interpret plural marriages in terms of our idiom of romantic love, according to which (ideally) a man and a woman have a lifelong, exclusive, and jealous attachment to one another.

Or take the case of Yanomamö warfare. The evidence of illegitimate coercion is overwhelming: the massacres and abductions clearly warrant disapproval according to the principle of coercion. This is true in spite of the suggestion that Yanomamö raiding is ecologically adaptive, for the analysis of the adaptive consequences of Yanomamö warfare is a hypothesis that may not be valid, and even if it is, why should the brutality that their warfare entails be preferable to periods of starvation?

The cross-cultural standard I am suggesting, that people ought to be free from illegitimate coercion, has the merit of being consistent with the main intent of the anthropologists' ethical relativism. It is tempting to go even farther and to suggest that the notion of freedom was both a primary motivation behind ethical relativism and its main justification, for the relativists seemed to think that their ethical theory was but an expression of the belief in the human right of self-determination. Kurt von Fritz has drawn a similar connection: he writes that, strangely enough, there is "a widespread belief that ethical relativism has a special affinity to 'democratic' or 'liberalistic' value systems" (1952:95).

Von Fritz and some other critics of ethical relativism have denied that one is justified in making a logical connection between the notions of freedom and ethical relativism. For example, von Fritz remarks that "historical experience" and "contemporary observation" show that "ethical relativism and totalitarian despotism go very well together" (1952:95; see also Schmidt 1955:786–87). They may be right that we are not led directly to the concept of freedom by the supposed fact that there are no general cross-cultural ethical principles. Yet the reverse does seem to hold: given the value of freedom, or the moral belief that people ought to be free to conduct their affairs as they choose, it follows that we ought to be tolerant of other ways of life.

The Boasians made a fateful choice in developing their notion of cultural freedom. They were so concerned that Western society not limit the freedom of others, and were so intent on the harm that had been inflicted by the more powerful nations on non-Western societies, that they ignored the suppression and violence in other civilizations. It is as if it is all right for someone else to engage in coercion, but not us.

Yet there are signs that the logic of their thought was pushing at least some of the ethical relativists in the direction that I am suggesting here. Ruth Benedict is illustrative. In 1947 Elgin Williams published a biting critique of her *Patterns of Culture.* He wrote the critique ostensibly because a new, twenty-five-cent edition of the book had just appeared, so it was now "available to the man on the street" (1947:84). Williams deplored the explicit message of the work—relativism and tolerance—and he felt it was time to correct it. The publication date of Williams' critique is significant, for World War II was recently over, and the war seems to have been a major challenge for ethical relativism, as we shall see, perhaps because it was difficult to regard the German invasion of Poland, or the execution of six million Jews, with much tolerance. Whatever the cause of his rebuke, Williams makes the point that "of course Dr. Benedict does not accept her theory any more than the other professors" (p. 86), for the call for tolerance is violated by her on page after page. For instance, she contrasts the response to marital infidelity among the Zuni and Plains Indians. The Plains husband cut off the fleshy part of his wife's nose if she was discovered committing adultery, whereas the Zuni husband responded without any violence whatever. Williams wrote:

> Can anyone read this and get the idea that Dr. Benedict regards Plains and Zuni behavior as equally valid? . . . Of course not. . . . She is definitely judging different ways of handling sex relations and we can set down her criterion tentatively: The presence or absence of violence. (1947:86)

Formally, Benedict sticks to relativism, yet "Try as she may to maintain the pose of relativism the test of consequences [or the use of value judgments] intrudes" (Williams 1947:88).

Benedict seems to have used a number of criteria in her evaluations, such as the criterion of happiness. The Zuni were "mildly happy" (1934a:262), whereas the Puritans of Colonial New England exhibited a strong "sense of guilt" (p. 276), and the "Puritan divines" spread considerable "suffering and frustration" about them (p. 277). Yet the presence or absence of coercion was a more frequent standard behind the value judgments that appear in her book. For example, Benedict pointedly discussed the virtues and defects of Zuni society (p. 246). A defect, she suggested, is that it does not offer much outlet for achievement or personal initiative, and consequently it lacks vigor. This culture is "incorrigibly mild." Yet on the positive side is that the people enjoy "freedom from any form of social exploitation or of social sadism." This is one of those societies which "is willing to live and let live"—or in which coercion is seldom used. To her, this was one of the great virtues of Zuni culture over Plains culture. On the other hand, the rivalry among the Kwakiutl Indians gave a "vigor and zest" to their lives that the Zuni lacked. But this was bought at high cost, which was a limitation of the peoples' freedom. Through the potlatch the chief sought to humiliate and bankrupt his rivals, and success was built on their ruin. This competition was a contest of power, "a tyranny from which . . . no man may free himself" (pp. 246–49). In discussing the witch-hunt of Salem, Benedict commented on the "confused and tormented women" who were put to death as witches; concerning the religious leaders, she says that seldom in any culture has there been "such complete intellectual and emotional dictatorship" (p. 276). These religious tyrants were so powerful they could cause the execution of almost anyone they chose.

Benedict's discussion of the abnormal in society is also illustrative (pp. 251–78). By the abnormal she meant the person whose natural inclinations or abilities run in a different direction from that in which the culture is moving, and who therefore is unrewarded, unsuccessful, and frustrated. An example is the homosexual who lives in a society in which homosexuality is regarded as a perversion. Benedict wrote that the homosexual's "guilt, his sense of inadequacy, his failures, are consequences of the disrepute which social tradition visits upon him, and few people can achieve a satisfactory life unsupported by the standards of their society" (p. 265). Here it is culture that does the tyrannizing—or more accurately the "normal" members of society do so in expressing their culture's values. And Benedict was not neutral about this tyranny, for she recommended tolerance toward those who deviate from the cultural standard. She even speculated that "It is probable that social orders of the future will carry this tolerance and encouragement of individual difference much further than any culture of which we have experience" (p. 273). The tyranny of tradition will eventually decline.

In sum, freedom from coercion may not have been the only criterion Benedict used when she expressed a more or less implicit evaluation of others, yet it was one of the primary ones.

Herskovits was less prone to allow value judgments of this kind to enter into his work. In one passage he discussed the benefits and disadvantages of European rule in West Africa. French and British governance brought material benefits, he remarked, and eliminated slavery, human sacrifice, and warfare; "it is thus possible for a man to live and trade where he will without fear of losing his personal liberty or his life." The African grants all this, yet he is still nostalgic about the past and looks forward to eventual freedom from European control. "There is, indeed, some reason to feel that the concept of freedom should be realistically defined as the right to be exploited in terms of the patterns of one's own culture" (1942, in 1973:9). Presumably Herskovits would have endorsed the violence of Yanomamö society. Yet in another passage written some years later, he seems to have been more equivocal. He posed the question whether we should show tolerance toward the ways of life of other people when these patterns include Soviet work-camps, the lynching of Negroes in the United States, and headhunting in Borneo. Herskovits remarked that "These are questions not easy to answer." "What we face," he suggested, "is the gigantic task of devising ways of dealing with man's inhumanity to man" (1956, in 1973:93–94). Apparently he was now willing at least to entertain the thought that coercion in other cultures could be criticized, that it need not command our tolerance and endorsement. Expressed somewhat differently, his call for absolute tolerance seems to have faltered as the issue of force in human affairs assumed greater prominence in his mind—perhaps as a result of the experiences of World War II.

CHAPTER SIX

A Growing Disaffection

HOW has relativism fared in anthropology during the last few decades? Not so well, it seems. In the 1970s the relativity of knowledge became a major topic of discussion in the anthropological literature (for example, Needham 1972), but its close cousin, ethical relativism, was almost universally rejected by the discipline. Certainly no one was carrying its banner the way Benedict and Herskovits did before they died (she in 1948, he in 1963).* In this chapter I will explain what has happened to ethical relativism since the beginning of World War II.

A number of developments both inside and out of anthropology worked against ethical relativism during the war and the years following. One was the war itself: in the face of world conflict, and especially of Nazism, the call for blanket tolerance seemed unreasonable. In 1938 Hitler annexed Austria, and in the months following he bullied his way to control over Czechoslovakia. In 1939 his army simply marched into Poland, which prompted Britain and France to declare war. The Nazi belief in Germany's racial superiority gave rise to some of the most gruesome policies the world had ever known, including the systematic annihilation of millions of Jews.

World War II was regarded by Americans as a conflict over ultimate values—democracy and freedom vs. tyranny and aggression. Not only was the one system of values viewed as a threat to the other, but even if it were not, even if Nazi Germany and the other Axis nations had been content with the land they occupied, the treatment of Czecho-

---

* For three relatively recent general discussions of ethical relativism in anthropology see Hanson 1975, Rudolph 1968, and Tennekes 1971.

slovakians, Poles, Jews, and others was simply too ghastly to tolerate. The problem was illustrated in anecdotal form by Abraham Edel (1955:16–17), a philosopher. He wrote of a historian who remarked in the early 1940s that he was ready to fight for his democratic values—to risk his own life and perhaps to take the lives of others in defense of his moral beliefs; nevertheless, the historian remarked, "nothing more could ultimately be said" for his own values "than for their Nazi opposites" (see also Cook 1978:310).

Elgin Williams' criticism of Ruth Benedict was mentioned earlier. His article was written just after World War II, and it trenchantly expressed the moral dilemma that the international conflict raised for ethical relativism. Williams wrote that the war experience was pervasive in the lives of the average citizen, and that it provided "the greatest mass education" in cultural differences the world had ever known (1947:84–85). And what was the lesson they learned? Surely the Gold Star Mother—a woman who had lost a son in the war effort—was not likely to grant that Hitler's culture was as valid as her own, no more than the survivors of Hiroshima were likely to show tolerance toward American generals, or the remaining European Jews to accept that there were two sides to the question of whether the Holocaust was appropriate.

World War II was a moral embarrassment to ethical relativism for two reasons. First, the question of the limits of our tolerance was forced on the discipline. Second, the war helped stimulate a sentiment that it may be possible after all to arrive at a set of ultimate values, such as those of freedom and humanity.

A second development at work against ethical relativism was the flush of optimism that spread across the Western world after the war was over. The historian Sidney Pollard (1968) has drawn a link between the rise of theories of progress on one hand and periods of optimism on the other. The belief in human improvement is an optimistic notion that has appeared in times of prosperity and hope: it grew during the optimism of the eighteenth-century Enlightenment, and waned during the pessimism of the early nineteenth century; it appeared again during the optimism of mid-to-late nineteenth century (the theories of Tylor and Spencer are representative) and waned again with the growing pessimism at the end of the century. The ethical relativism of the Boasians by this analysis was a manifestation of late nineteenth- and early twentieth-century pessimism. Yet the period following World War II was one of renewed optimism (Pollard 1968:186–87). The side of freedom and democracy won the war after all, and then the victorious nations set about to reconstruct the very countries they had so recently fought. Both Germany and Japan not only recovered, but did so with democratic governments and booming economies. This was also a time of material prosperity, and the non-Western peoples of Africa, Asia, South America, the Pacific, and elsewhere, were now sharing some of the benefits that formerly had been reserved for the industrialized countries: "Put at its crudest, the haves can afford to give something away, and the have-nots can see improvements ahead even in the existing framework" (p. 187).

The historical experience (to use Pollard's phrase) was now favorable for the return of the idea of progress, or for the idea that something good can be said for civilization. The condition of modern society may not be so absurd after all. It is reasonable to suggest further that the mood was set for a more optimistic view about values, one which holds that it may be possible to arrive at moral principles which can legitimately be applied across cultural boundaries—values, say, the discovery of which may contribute to the achievement of international understanding and world peace.

A third development working against ethical relativism was a growing interest within the discipline in achieving scientific regularities, or broad theory, in the study of cultures (Hatch 1973b). Boasian anthropologists had been a-theoretical if not anti-theoretical almost from the beginning (Kluckhohn 1939). Once the data were gathered in sufficient quantity, it was believed, theory would emerge almost by itself. By the late 1920s, however, signs of impatience began to appear, and by the late 1930s—certainly by the time World War II began—this impatience had turned into an outright attack on the empirical rigidity and theoretical austerity of Boas. A new mood had come over American anthropology, a mood that sought desperately for theoretical innovation. One anthropologist (White 1939:573) expressed the growing sentiment with the comment, "What we need in American ethnology today is not additional facts, but interpretations of the facts we already possess in abundance."

Perhaps this development was not unrelated to world affairs. The general pessimism of the 1920s, the worldwide economic collapse of the 1930s, and World War II stimulated a sense of crisis within the discipline. The world was in trouble, deep trouble, and the best anthropologists could do in response, it seemed, was to gather coyote tales and moccasin designs. What was needed was a scientific understanding of humanity that the world could use and that would distinguish the discipline.

The growing concern in anthropology for general, scientific principles brought a spate of methodological and theoretical developments. This began modestly at first in the late 1920s, but it was fully underway by the 1940s. Included among the innovations was culture and personality research, which focused on the relationship between culture and the human personality system and included such problems as the role of cultural institutions in the reduction of tension. Another innovation was acculturation research, which sought to understand the impact of Western society on non-Western peoples and concentrated on such matters as the frustration and patterns of resistance and accommodation exhibited by the societies that were dominated. A third was cultural ecology, which set out to discover general patterns of cultural adaptation to environmental conditions.

Against this general background of developments—the moral implications of World War II, the growing optimism of the postwar years, and the strong interest in achieving broad theory and generalizations—we can understand that the conviction began to emerge among American anthropologists, including some of the most eminent, during roughly the late 1940s and the 1950s, that universal values or moral absolutes can be found. The notion of moral absolutes was conceived on the order of scientific generalizations that were to emerge from a systematic analysis of the data.

Ralph Linton is illustrative. In the 1950s he was arguing that a close look at the evidence reveals not a condition of almost infinite variety in the sphere of morals, but rather the recurrence of certain common standards of value in societies all over the world. Linton remarked that "the first impression which one receives from the study of a series of unrelated cultures is one of almost unlimited variety" (1952:646). Nevertheless, he continued, "Behind the seemingly endless diversity of culture patterns" (and here he included values) "there is a fundamental uniformity." Linton had an encyclopedic grasp of world ethnography: he had read extensively in the literature and his retention was remarkable, and in this article he wanted to summarize some of the regularities in ethical principles that he thought he could make out. For instance, he suggested that in all societies parents are morally obligated to care for their children and to train them, while the children are expected to care for their parents when they become old (p. 653). In all societies, he noted, "some degree of loyalty and mutual assistance is prescribed" between siblings, although the extent of this support varies widely among cultures (p. 654). Nearly all peoples who live under conditions which do not allow the accumulation of material goods have patterns whereby food is shared and tools and weapons are freely lent (p. 656). All societies are set up in such a fashion that individual interests are made subordinate at some point to the needs of the larger whole (p. 659). And violence is condemned everywhere, although there are cultural differences in its definition (pp. 659–60).

Linton did not present these conclusions as a matter of dispassionate scientific interest, for he had a very practical goal in mind. He suggested that the "resemblances in ethical concepts" among human societies provided a "sound basis for mutual understanding" (p. 660) and a major step toward world peace (see also Linton 1954:166–68), for these common moral principles constitute a basis for the establishment of universal standards of right and wrong.*

The view also emerged after the war that even where we do not find ethical universals, some values can be valued more highly than others. Clyde Kluckhohn suggested that cultural values are not of equal validity; for instance, values which deny the common humanity of all men,

---

* The logical flaw of Linton's suggestion should be apparent from what was said in an earlier chapter. The fact that every society in the world embraces a given moral norm does not elevate that norm to an ultimate good. Linton's error was to try to derive a moral principle from a factual state of affairs. See Taylor 1958.

and which deny the right of some men to be treated as persons, are unsatisfactory (1955:675). Similarly, Redfield suggested that although the "contents" of moral systems around the world may be quite divergent, nevertheless, values tend "to vary around basic similarities" (1953:159–69). The mores may have the capacity "to make anything right," and hence to vary radically among societies, yet it is easier to make some patterns of behavior more right than others. Hence some moral patterns are more common, even if not universal. For example, "I am sure that the mores have an easier time making it right for mothers to cherish their children . . . than they have to make it right for a mother to cherish her child and then eat it." Similarly, he notes that "the cold cruelty of the Nazis, or cannibalism within the in-group," diverge from the general trend of human values. His point was that values which diverge from the norm (like those contained in Nazism) run counter to some general standard of good. They are not as fitting and valid as the more humane moral principles that are widely though perhaps not universally shared.

Redfield and at least one other leading American anthropologist, A. L. Kroeber, went even farther (see also Ginsberg 1953). They suggested not only that there are general standards of judgment that transcend cultural boundaries, but that the moral standing of primitive societies is below that of civilizations like the United States and China. An ethical transformation has occurred from the primitive or precivilized level to that of civilization. This idea is quite significant, for it amounts to a reintroduction of the concept of moral progress.

Redfield developed this theme by posing the question whether we "judge a primitive culture by the same standards by which [we] judge Russia or the United States" (1953:157). He suggested that we do not: we have lower moral expectations for the simpler societies, hence we are less critical of them. For example, we do not expect them to protect freedom of thought the same as we do the higher civilizations, so we do not fault them for subjugation and repression the way we do Russia or the United States. Again, we do not condemn the Siriono husband who leaves his wife alone to die in the jungle the same as we do the suburban husband who leaves his wife to die in a snowdrift (p. 163). Redfield suggested that because we use a double standard of

judgment, our understanding of the moral transformation that has occurred from primitive to civilized societies has been obscured: since
we are not as judgmental toward the primitives, we fail to recognize
that their standards on the whole are less humane.

In Redfield's view this moral difference between primitive and civilized people is not due to some ethical dereliction on the part of the
simpler societies. Their standards may not be as worthy, but the people themselves are not to blame. I think Redfield's position was that
the values of primitive societies reflect the very different conditions
under which they live. For example, the Siriono man abandons his
dying spouse in the jungle because of the rigors of life; he has no
practical choice (see p. 140). "We do not expect a people to have a
moral norm that their material conditions of life make impossible" (p.
163). Yet even though the people themselves are not to blame, this
does not make their values any more acceptable. Because of their values the people exhibit less moral sensitivity, hence more brutality,
violence, and cruelty.

Redfield was not very precise about the criterion he used in judging
good and bad (and in distinguishing primitive and civilized values),
but by listing some of the practices he approved and disapproved it is
possible to give some idea what he had in mind. He told the story of
a Pawnee chief and his son who tried to bring an end to human sacrifice among their people. According to Pawnee belief, a person captured in warfare, normally a young woman, had to be sacrificed in
order to ensure the crops. The young man in question and his father
were so repelled by the brutality of the ritual that they went against
public opinion and risked their own safety in trying to free a succession of prisoners who were about to be slain (pp. 130–33, 136–40).
In Redfield's discussion this story symbolized the moral transformation
that he believed took place. Sacrifice is inhumane and can legitimately be disapproved, whereas the attempts to save the young victims
warrant praise.

Similarly, Redfield (following Kroeber) disapproved of such practices as the use of torture as a judicial procedure, beatings as a form
of punishment, and slaughtering prisoners of war (p. 162). He described an incident he observed in Yucatan, Mexico; some of his Mayan

friends caught a wild animal, doused it with gasoline, and burned it alive. Redfield condemned the act as lacking kindness and compassion (p. 164). He also disapproved head-hunting and cannibalism (p. 148). Civilized societies came in for criticism. Redfield found fault with white supremacy in Mississippi, the political policy in Russia with its "dehumanizing, fear-ridden way of life," and the Nazis (pp. 148–49). Civilized morals may be more refined, but they have hardly reached perfection.

The ethical principle that Redfield saw in the moral transformation from primitive to civilized society, and which he used in making judgments of good and bad, is the principle of decency and humaneness (pp. 163, 164). It is good to treat people (and animals) with respect and kindness, to look after their welfare, to avoid causing them pain and suffering.

Kroeber suggested that there are also other differences between primitive and civilized cultures besides an increasing humaneness, and he referred to these collectively as manifestations of progress: he remarked that even though we are justly critical of the old-fashioned, nineteenth-century idea of evolution, "there can be no doubt that there has occurred, since Paleolithic times, a great deal of some kind of progress in culture, and a fairly continuous progress at that" (1952:318). The crux of the problem, then, is to determine in what ways culture has progressed, and he suggested that there are four (1948:296–304, 1952:318).

First, there has been a growth in the sheer quantity of culture traits: small-scale, hunting and gathering societies normally have only a fraction of the cultural inventory of modern societies. The "sum total of [the] culture of mankind has pretty continuously grown in bulk through history" (1948:297).

Second, Kroeber suggested a decline in magic and supernaturalism (p. 299). The simpler societies accept as effective and real certain phenomena and procedures which are rejected in the more advanced cultures. For instance, the simpler societies accept dreams as premonitions of the future, and believe that slight mental derangements like trance and delusions are results of supernatural forces. Among us, someone who believes he hears the dead speaking to him or who is convinced he can turn himself into a bear or wolf is considered to be mentally unsound, but among primitives this same person is thought to have special powers which he may use for good or evil. This is not to say that a belief in God is a sign of backwardness, he added. What he was referring to rather is a failure to distinguish between subjective experiences, like hallucinations, and objective phenomena, or a tendency to ascribe supernatural significance to mild mental derangements (1948:300, 1952:318).

Third is that in primitive cultures physiological or anatomical matters are drawn into social affairs more than among civilized peoples. For example, women may be put into seclusion during menstruation; people may become preoccupied with the body of a dead person, the widow wearing the jaw bone of the deceased strung around her neck; the bodies of the living may be subjected to mutilation—the head may be deformed by binding it tightly with strips of cloth, the front teeth may be knocked out. It is in this context that Kroeber considered the simpler cultures less humane: they are more given to torture, sacrifice, and the like. The major world religions like Buddhism and Christianity have progressively excluded such brutality and have come to sanction more humane behavior.

The fourth element of progress, he suggested, occurs in the domain of technology, mechanics, and science. Inventions in this sphere are not easily forgotten, hence they tend to accumulate in progressive fashion. Complex societies have more effective techniques, tools, machines, technical knowledge, and the like.

These discussions about moral absolutes and moral progress—Redfield's and Kroeber's ideas about the improvements that come with civilization, and the attempts of Linton and others to sift the ethnographic literature to discover universal values—stopped almost as abruptly as they began. By the 1960s this general line of thinking had virtually ceased. In part, perhaps, this was because the postwar optimism had faded with the 1960s. The major cities in the United States— New York, Los Angeles, and Detroit, among others—experienced growing racial tension which finally erupted in uncontrollable riots in the black ghettos. The environment was suffering a crisis of another order, chiefly pollution, making most urban centers both unpleasant and unhealthy, and no one knew what to do about it. The Vietnam War grew in scale, and yet it seemed unwinnable; then dissent over the war culminated in more riots, reaching the Democratic National Convention in Chicago and igniting campuses around the country. The American Anthropological Association itself was torn apart from inside over what it should or should not do in speaking out against the war. When the nation's faith in its leadership seemed to be at its lowest, the President of the United States became involved in one of the most serious controversies ever to touch the White House, the Watergate break-in; facing the possibility of impeachment proceedings, Nixon resigned in disgrace. In short, perhaps the "historical experience" now provided too uncongenial a milieu for the growth of the optimistic idea that civilization represents moral improvement, or that human beings here or anywhere have the high-mindedness to establish moral principles of wide validity in their cultures and then to follow them in their lives.

Yet the concept of progress has not disappeared from the anthropologist's lexicon by any means, for it still appears reasonably often in the works of those who are interested in cultural ecology. I need to describe this current use of the term in some detail, for it illustrates very effectively how thinking about moral absolutes and moral improvement withered in American anthropology.

Cultural ecologists are concerned with the cultural adjustments to the physical world, which in turn imply progress: cultures by this approach are seen from the perspective of their progressive adaptation through time. Because cultural ecology includes both the time dimension and a focus on adaptation it has become closely associated with cultural evolution, and cultural ecologists usually identify themselves as cultural evolutionists. A typical theme in the work of the evolutionists is the attempt to rank societies according to a single scale of development (see for example Fried 1967; Service 1971), and Western society is explicitly conceived as occupying a higher position on the scale than, say, the Trobriand Islanders or Pawnee Indians. Yet it is not assumed that this hierarchy represents improvement. This is illustrated by one of the most frequently cited works in the literature on cultural evolution, an article by Marshall Sahlins that was published in 1960.

Sahlins distinguished between two levels at which cultural evolution can be viewed. First is the perspective of specific evolution, from which we see a process of differentiation. In specific evolution, cultures become specialized by adapting to particular local conditions, primarily environmental ones, and since these vary widely, cultures are diverse. He drew a connection between this environmentally rooted pattern of cultural diversity and the Boasian view about the selectivity of cultures (1960:26). Whereas the Boasians described the differences among peoples as fortuitous and unexplainable, Sahlins suggested rather that they should be seen as adaptive specializations, for human institutions are adjusted and changed according to adaptational requirements. He commented that culture "is man's means of adaptation," for it "provides the technology for appropriating nature's energy and putting it to service, as well as the social and ideological means of implementing the process." In short, "Cultures are organizations for doing something, for perpetuating human life and themselves."* Specific evolution then is the specific adaptation of a culture to the local environment: "as the problems of survival vary, cultures accordingly change," and thus cultures undergo "phylogenetic, adaptive development" (p. 24).

At the level of specific evolution, according to Sahlins, the principle of relativity holds, because each culture adapts to a unique set of circumstances. The Eskimo kinship system is adapted to the necessities of life in that region and cannot be evaluated as higher or lower than, say, the kinship system of the Crow Indians. Cultural features should be evaluated as more or less successful only in relation to the environment in which they occur and not according to some absolute standard. Sahlins wrote that each culture "is adequate in its own way, given the adaptive problems confronted and the available means of meeting them." And "what is selectively advantageous for one [culture] may be simply ruinous for another." Nor is it true that cultures which might be considered higher in general evolutionary standing necessarily are better adapted to their specific environments than the

---

* Sahlins has radically altered his views about the role of culture as an adaptive resource. See Sahlins 1977.

lower cultures. "Many great civilizations," he writes, "have fallen in the last 2,000 years, . . . while the Eskimos tenaciously maintained themselves in an incomparably more difficult habitat" (pp. 26–27). The second level at which we may view evolution is the general level. In spite of the individual differences among cultures, societies can be ranked in a single hierarchy, and since the higher forms developed later than the lower ones the hierarchy has a temporal dimension. Considered at the level of specific evolution, a study of warfare in different societies would lead to an understanding of different adaptive pressures in various parts of the world and the different kinds of warfare that exist, but warfare can also be viewed in general terms, for the various forms of warfare can be ranked according to such features as the amount of resources deployed and the number of persons involved. We discover such developments as "increase in the scale of war, in the size of armies and the numbers of casualties, in the duration of campaigns, and the significance of outcome for the survival of the societies involved." These trends are explained not by reference to the adaptation of cultures to local conditions, but in terms of the general development of other features of the culture to which warfare is related, "such as increasing economic productivity or the emergence of special political institutions" (p. 30). At the level of general evolution, Sahlins suggests, we are not relativists at all, for we rank societies as higher and lower; we are noting cultural progress (p. 27).

What are the criteria for progress? The amount of energy harnessed is one, for higher civilizations have means for harnessing energy (like the internal combustion engine, hydroelectric turbines, and nuclear reactors) that the simpler societies can hardly imagine (pp. 33–35). Closely linked to this is a second, an even more useful criterion: levels of integration, especially of social organization; societies can be ranked according to degrees of complexity—bands, tribes, chiefdoms, and states (pp. 35–37). Third, progress can be seen "as improvement in 'all-round adaptability' " (p. 37). Higher cultures are more powerful than lower ones and come to dominate them, and are also less restricted to specific environments so that they can spread. Sahlins wrote: "General cultural evolution, to summarize, is passage from less to greater energy transformation, lower to higher levels of integration, and less to greater all-round adaptability" (p. 38). Yet Sahlins did not suggest that progress necessarily implied improvement or a higher level of existence for mankind. He did not think it brought greater happiness, nor more secure, fulfilling, or enjoyable lives for the citizens of the civilized nations. In some respects it may do so: medical care and knowledge of nutrition may have improved, for example. On the other hand, modern warfare is far more destructive than the primitive forms. Another cultural evolutionist, Elman Service, has expressed the same view (in conversation). He defines progress as movement along a line, or as a form of directionality. For example, a person says that a boil on the neck is progressing—which in this instance means it is getting worse, not better.

The point of view of writers like Service and Sahlins illustrates what has happened to the notion of moral progress in American anthropology. The budding ideas about moral absolutes and improvement that were associated chiefly with the 1950s seem to have been too delicate to survive the pessimistic environment of the 1960s and later.

Leslie White was one of the main advocates of cultural evolutionism in twentieth-century American anthropology, and a change that came about in his thinking is another illustration of the withering effects of the new pessimism. Even before the 1950s White's evolutionism had a strongly optimistic bent. In a classic statement he wrote that the "purpose and function of culture are to make life secure and enduring for the human species," and evolution for him meant increasing security and material prosperity for human beings (1959:8). His evolutionism included a strong functionalist component, and he argued that institutions like religious ritual and incest taboos have unintended and beneficial effects (they serve our interests) even without our knowing it. This very sanguine conception of human institutions changed abruptly at some point between 1973 and 1975 (White 1975:9), however, when he came to the opinion that culture does not serve the interests of mankind at all, for it is oriented rather toward its own perpetuation. Institutions function to maintain the cultural system, and they may do great harm to human beings in the process. A culture that is highly stable and viable may be miserable to live in. White tells how he came to this change of view (1975:12). His earlier, optimistic thinking reflected the work that he was doing on the evolution of primitive societies which, he felt, did indeed have a benevolent quality. At the primitive level, culture can be seen as "the benevolent custodian of a mankind." But White shifted his attention to complex civilization later in his career, which forced him to rethink his ideas about a pattern of general improvement in history. He wrote that although cultural systems do provide mankind with such benefits and necessities as food and a knowledge of fire with which to cook it, and dwellings for protection from the weather, they have also resulted in the slaughter of millions of people in warfare, the torture and killing of countless others in inquistions, and the burning of still more as witches (1975:10–11). Cultural systems have brought urban congestion, slavery, and serfdom. No crime is too heinous that it will not be stimulated by cultural systems, which "have encouraged and rewarded the manufacture and sale of adulterated or contaminated food, and dangerous, even lethal, drugs." What is more, "Culture put young children to work in textile mills for fifteen hours a day, begat sweat shops that consumed the lives of impecunious women who had no alternatives but starvation or prostitution." The optimism of White's earlier cultural evolutionism may have seemed too robust to succumb, yet eventually it did so.

One might think that the searing effect of pessimism on the notions about moral absolutes and human improvement would lead to a regeneration of ethical relativism, but this did not happen, for still other forces were at work, forces that were entirely separate from the ones considered so far. Beginning just before World War II, and increasing rapidly afterward, especially in the 1960s, the criticism was heard that cultural relativism is not as benign as had been believed. The view was growing that it contains an insidious bias toward the status quo and in favor of the preservation of foreign or exotic cultures, as human zoos, or as anthropological specimens. This bias often is patently undesirable and unwanted by the very people whose freedom it is supposed to protect. In the mid-1960s a British anthropologist, Lucy Mair, wrote that anthropologists then were often "more interested in identifying the obstacles" standing in the way of change, "in the hope of trying to remove them," than in trying to protect the exotic cultures of the world from Western influence (1965:440). This was a radical shift for the discipline to make.

At least three factors were behind this development. First, the experience since the war has been that non-Western or Third World peoples by and large have wanted change to a far greater extent than the earlier anthropologists realized. A dramatic example is the case of Manus, one of the Admiralty Islands in the Pacific. The people of Manus were studied in the late 1920s by Margaret Mead, who returned again in the 1950s (Mead 1956). It seems that the society had been transformed during the interim, and that this had taken place with reasonable ease and the almost complete willingness of the people. Mead was explicit about the implications of her Manus findings for cultural relativism (pp. 436–45). She raised the question of what our ethical attitude should be with respect to changing other peoples— where should we stand on the question of bringing "civilization" to them?

Until about 1940, she wrote (perhaps autobiographically), the view prevailed among American anthropologists that we should respect the dignity of native cultures, and when a lecturing anthropologist was asked if the Balinese wanted progress, the answer was, "Progress to what?" Balinese culture is good in itself, so why should they want to become like us? After World War II, she noted, new developments were underway, although the anthropologist was slow to see them. In trying to protect primitive peoples from changes that were not wanted, the anthropologist failed to see that changes they did want were being denied. After World War II many non-Western peoples began "clamoring for the blessings of the modern world, machine technology, universal literacy, [and] medicine" (p. 442), yet much of the Western world was not responsive, the anthropologists included. Anthropologists, she noted, "were still trapped in a one-sided picture" that when changes took place in foreign societies it was because "something was being *done* to [the] people" (p. 442).

It is true, she suggested, that foreign societies do not always jump at the chance to improve themselves. For example, tribal peoples may turn restless and refuse to work for wages, and they may not take care of the houses provided for them. Mead explained that this may be a response on their part like that of the bright girl among us who seems unable to learn physics and to lack ambition. This is not due to some intrinsic incapacity, but comes about because the young woman sees little chance of advancement: in our society girls do not become physicists—by convention. Similarly, the aspiring native realizes he can not move above the ranks of manual labor and will forever be a second-class citizen, so he quits striving.

Mead's experience in Manus was not an isolated one by any means, for extremely few people anywhere in the world have not actively sought at least some of the products of industrialization. For example, primitives want steel knives over traditional stone blades. They recognize the value of steel wool in cleaning cooking pots, and the superiority of metal tins over earthen jars for carrying water. Women who spend several hours a day grinding grain for the evening meal have good reason to prefer flour that is ground at a mill. Horticulturalists usually want at least some cash crop for the income it brings to buy manufactured goods. Possibly they also look forward to acquiring running water and a surfaced road to the nearest town. It is not only the utilitarian items and innovations that are wanted, for high on the list of priorities commonly are such treasures as transistor radios, television sets, and electric guitars, while the educated and more affluent are often interested in such items as large automobiles and fancy refrigerators stocked with expensive food.

This is not to say that all societies are rushing headlong into Westernization and modernization, for many have indeed preferred to keep their traditional ways and to accept only a few items from the industrialized nations. Some of the Andaman Islanders, for one, have avoided contact with outsiders, and some of the Hopi villages have sought to maintain much of their traditional culture even though they live in the midst of American society. Non-Western peoples are also selective in what they are interested in, as a rule; the people want what they consider the best of Western patterns and to keep much of their own way of life intact. What is more, non-Western peoples often show ambivalence about the changes that occur; ambivalence of this kind is a recurrent theme of Third World novels, for example (David Brokensha, personal communication).

The desire for change—more precisely, for economic, social, and political development—is especially manifest in the emergence of new, Third World nations. After World War II one colonial dependency after another gained autonomy: India, Indonesia, Lebanon, the Philippines, the Sudan, and others. The nationalistic aspirations of the non-Western world were growing, and the war had jarred power relations enough that independence could be won. More or less reluctantly, the Western powers had to accept the changes: the age of colonialism was over.

The new nations have exhibited a robust sense of nationalism, which in turn is associated with a very strong drive for development. These countries by and large have wanted to be included in the community of nations and the world economy—or at least this is true of their ruling classes. They have sought to improve agricultural production, to acquire the benefits of industrialization like medicine and helicopters, and to build factories. Generally they have tried to change at a much faster pace than was permitted under colonial rule, and they often have the sense that they were (and still are) being denied both full membership in the world community and the material benefits of industrialization and development. There is some truth to these views.

The focus on development and change at the national level in Third World countries has led to a serious dilemma for those in the West with an international interest in human rights and welfare. Small pockets of hunter-gatherers, semi-nomadic pastoralists, and conservative agriculturalists have not always wanted to accept the innovations that their new leaders have prescribed. In Tanzania, for example, the Maasai have been very slow to change, and as a result pressure has been brought by the government to induce them to accept modernization and to join the nation in its quest for development. Third World governments at times have used force to bring about change; and whether motivated by a desire for modernization or simply by prejudice, some national leaders have shown little reluctance to engage in genocidal practices toward what are usually the poorer and more "backward" minorities within their countries' borders. A striking case is the Montagnards, who have been despised and exploited by the dominant Vietnamese for generations. Almost from the time the Republic of South Vietnam was formed in the 1950s it was deemed to be in the national interest to assimilate and civilize the Montagnard people, who were considered savages by the government. Many of the Montagnards were driven from their land, which was redistributed to Vietnamese. It was decreed that their language would not be taught at school nor used in any official context. Montagnard names for streets, villages, and towns were changed to Vietnamese, and Montagnard soldiers and employees had to take Vietnamese names. In one province Montagnard dress was prohibited, and in another the Montagnards were forced to build their houses in Vietnamese fashion. Their leaders were kept out of government and at times were imprisoned; the Montagnards were given inferior health care, and their legal rights were ignored; it was believed that Montagnards were thrown into prison at the whim of the police, and that when they served in the army they were given the hardest and most dangerous work. Being uprooted from their land many were forced to live as refugees, and during the Vietnam War thousands were killed by bombs, disease, and hunger (MRG 1974).

The dilemma which cases like this create for people in the fully industrialized countries is patent. The humanitarian in Europe or North America, say, is led to oppose the actions, beliefs, and values of Third World governments when the latter are pursuing what they consider to be national interests. A number of organizations have appeared in the industrialized countries in an attempt to protect minorities in the Third World (and elsewhere) by publicizing their plight. Examples are the International Work Group for Indigenous Affairs, centered in Copenhagen; Cultural Survival, with offices in Cambridge, Massachusetts; Amnesty International, and the Minority Rights Group (MRG), both of which have headquarters in London. The Minority Rights Group is illustrative. Privately funded, its principal aims are to promote the rights and welfare of minority peoples throughout the world by monitoring their condition, conducting detailed studies of specific cases in which human rights are violated, and publicizing its findings. It has produced reports on such topics as the position of blacks in Brazil, the Chinese in Indonesia, the Montagnards of South Vietnam, and Mexican-Americans in the United States (for example, see Marnham 1977; MRG 1974).

A second factor behind the anthropologist's turn of mind on the question of change is that it has become clear that great harm may come to societies that stay as they are, a point that was made quite forcefully with regard to Indonesia by Raymond Kennedy in 1943. Indonesia had been colonized by the Dutch, who in some ways were quite tolerant, considerate, and benevolent in their rule, according to Kennedy. They did not impose their own law, for example, but set up a legal system which incorporated the customary law of the local peoples. They instituted a system of property-holding whereby land could not be bought by outsiders, hence the indigenous population was protected from expropriation by European interests. The Dutch colonial service was made up almost entirely of anthropologists who were sensitive to the native point of view and who worked with great care to preserve the native cultures. And what was the effect? It was "an Indonesia so far behind the times that it is helpless unless protected by some strong, modern, outside power" (p. 188).

The motivation behind the very benevolent policy of the Dutch may also be suspect, Kennedy suggested. The financial imperialists have a vested interest in avoiding the economic betterment of the indigenous peoples, for economic development creates a demand for higher wages and improved public welfare. The relativists' policy of encouraging "primitivism" and of maintaining tribal heterogeneity, it would seem, is in perfect harmony with the interests of capitalist exploitation. The relativists' policy of cultural preservation also minimizes the cost of colonial administration: very little has to be spent on schools, for example, if there is no demand for formal education.

Part of the problem is that few if any societies can be truly independent under present circumstances, because world affairs touch virtually every part of the globe. Elizabeth Colson remarks that in forty years as an anthropologist (and a very active field ethnographer at that) not once has she encountered a primitive: she has never studied "any group that was isolated from the impact of world events or . . . that was not part of some larger system." She cites the case of bridewealth payments in central Africa. Fluctuations in bridewealth have been linked to the world economy as far back as one can tell. The nature and quantity of goods changing hands "reflect[ed] the depression of the 1930s, the demands for local labor and produce during World War II, and the inflation of the past decade." What is more, such matters as wages and the price of fish, maize, livestock, and other goods are of urgent interest even to the very isolated peoples of Africa, "including the Gwembe Tonga of what was then Northern Rhodesia whose villages in 1949 were along the Zambezi River some two days walk from the nearest shop—there was no road—and who depended almost entirely on local resources for food, clothing, and equipment" (1976:262). People everywhere are inevitably subjected to outside influences, and consequently they are vulnerable.

A third factor was involved in the anthropologist's more favorable attitude toward change. As a whole, anthropologists have grown less relativistic in their thinking about the material welfare of human beings, so they are more inclined to use this as a standard in evaluating a people's condition and as a justification for change.

Relativists like Benedict held that cultures vary all but randomly with respect to practical matters and that institutions frequently fly in the face of reason. In this sense hers was an irrational version of culture (see Hatch 1973a:86–91). An example is her discussion of Kurnai marriage patterns, described in an earlier chapter. Ralph Linton expressed a similar view in the 1930s. He remarked that a society which for generations has existed on hand labor, focusing its attention on matters other than economic or practical considerations, "will feel no great urge to adopt labor-saving appliances, even those which exhibit a high degree of efficiency" (1936:321). The anthropologists in the 1930s also held that these patterns in other cultures are equally valid. For example, Benedict implied that although our society places an emphasis on economic and material considerations, we should not mistake this for a universal standard (1934a:36).

After the war, however, the view became more pronounced that the range of variability in the sphere of practical interests is not as great, or that cultural orientations are not quite as random, as the relativists of the 1930s believed. For example, George Murdock wrote that he "felt increasingly uncomfortable about the concept of relativity" for some years (1965:144), and that it is absurd to suggest that all cultural usages are equally valid and deserve equal respect (p. 149). He suggested that certain patterns of life are better than others on purely practical grounds, and that the peoples of exotic societies share this evaluation:

> Ethnography demonstrates that, when faced with expanded possibilities of cultural choice, all peoples reveal a preference for steel over stone axes, for quinine and penicillin over magical therapy, for money over barter, for animal and vehicular transport over human porterage, for improvements in the food supply which enable them to rear their children and support their aged rather than killing them, and so on. They relinquish cannibalism and head-hunting with little resistance when colonial governments demonstrate the material advantages of peace. (p. 149)

What is more, a "revolution of rising expectations" is occurring throughout most of the world (p. 150)—a desire to enjoy at least some of the material advantages that industrialization has to offer. Ian Hogbin remarks that anthropologists once were unrealistic and sentimental in deploring the changes taking place in primitive societies, but that the "modern anthropologists have a different attitude." He continues:

> They know of the losses that change has brought in its train; but they also see the gains. Tribal conflict probably had all the merits that were claimed for it, yet now that peace has been established travel is easier, and goods and ideas can be freely exchanged. Anthropologists of today accept the fact that Western technology and Western ways are spreading over the face of the globe, and it is they who have revealed that in many places the native is already more eager to accept than the European is to give. (1958:39)

In an article on anthropology and development, George Dalton remarks that

The glaring fact of the underdeveloped world is its material poverty. . . . Poverty means not only insufficient food, but also disease, early death, and a life sentence of ignorance, immobility, and meanness for hundreds of millions of people. (1971:5, see also pp. 26–29)

Conrad Arensberg and Arthur Niehoff write:

There is evidence that men in all stages of culture have been interested in acquiring whatever new things and techniques would benefit them in a practical way, but the desire for such improvements was probably never at such a pitch or on such a worldwide scale as it is today. Satisfaction with the old way of life, at least as measured by material goods, is rarely found in the modern world. (1971:200–201)

In brief, a general (but not unanimous) consensus seems to have formed that the material well-being of people is a value that can be applied across cultural boundaries. We can legitimately regard it as bad that a people have an insecure existence, and we can reasonably want to improve their material condition. This leads logically to the notion of economic development.

The period since World War II has seen considerable effort and money directed toward the study and promotion of development in the Third World. Both the Ford and Rockefeller foundations, for example, have sponsored programs of research, and such organizations as the United States Agency for International Development (AID) and the World Bank have mobilized expertise and resources to help bring about change. Anthropologists have been active in contributing studies and helping to implement projects, and the topic of development has become important within the discipline. Yet attitudes about development have changed since the immediate postwar years, and this itself throws light on the value held by anthropologists about the well-being of human societies. The change, in brief, is that by the 1970s at least, it had become clear that most development programs do not work very well; some specialists now were even saying that they were an utter failure. In particular, it became clear that the gap between the rich and poor nations was growing and not diminishing. When development did occur it often took place at the expense of the poor: in the developing countries there emerged an elite which prospered, enjoying increasing power and wealth, while the less fortunate became even worse off than before, sometimes being exploited by their more privileged countrymen in a way that rivaled the conditions of colonial rule. One writer remarked that in spite of "the massive injections of 'aid' into the underdeveloped countries"—aid that was "recommended as a result of [social science] studies"—nevertheless, " 'development' and 'modernization' are not taking place, except [among] a limited elite" (Hill 1975:31).

The framework by which development and modernization were conceived after World War II by and large consisted of a single continuum: at one end are the fully developed nations like the United States, at the other are the underdeveloped ones like Mali, and at various points in-between are such countries as Mexico. If the developing nations are given sufficient material assistance and advice, it was assumed, and if they use this help wisely, they will move up the scale toward the pole of full economic development and economic independence. Yet the developmental scale itself was soon called into question: it became clear that aid does not necessarily propel Third World countries in the direction of the industrialized nations and often only serves to make them even more dependent than before on their rich benefactors. In addition, the lesson from at least some cases was that "development" leads to the general disintegration of the local economy.

The case of the Sahel, a semi-arid region forming the southern border of the Sahara desert, is illustrative (Marnham 1977). Originally it was peopled by semi-nomadic tribal societies whose economic and social systems were adapted to drought conditions. In recent decades a number of large-scale development programs were undertaken there, the goal being to settle the wandering peoples, increase the productivity of their herds, and draw them into the world economy. In addition, programs were undertaken to build roads, dig deep wells, develop irrigation, and establish a sedentary farming population. The effects were quite different from what was expected: what happened was that the environment became degraded due to overpopulation and overgrazing, a need was created for some form of continuing outside aid, and there emerged a sizable number of refugees living in poverty and dependency. Questions have also been raised about the intentions of those who promoted development in the Sahel: the programs for improvement may have been designed to serve the interests of the sedentary people at the expense of the poorer and less powerful pastoralists, for example.

The lesson the Sahel suggests to some anthropologists is that development may best be conceived not as a single continuum, with all economic systems eventually becoming copies of the industrial model; but rather as a pluralistic process which leads in different directions according to the circumstances. For example, it may be possible to improve the conditions of life among the native peoples of the Sahel by giving them both technical and technological assistance, better breeds of cattle, medical facilities, a more secure water supply, and the like, but without trying to turn them into ranchers and farmers living in towns and engaging in capital-intensive, high-technology systems of production. Development need not entail "growth" in the Western sense.

A pluralistic conception of development such as this bears a certain resemblance to Boasian relativism, for both assume that change proceeds in various directions and that the modes of life of peoples around the world are fundamentally diverse. Yet there is a difference: the pluralistic view of development holds that values are not completely relative, for it assumes that all people share a common and very basic desire to be reasonably well-off. The people of the Sahel may not want to discard their way of life for the American one, but like us they want to pursue their life goals with comfort and security. What is more, this principle of material well-being constitutes a standard of judgment: development in the Sahel is judged a failure by the same standard that justified attempts by AID and others to try it in the first place. A pluralistic conception of development does not imply a relativity of values at all, but rather a diversity of means to achieve a secure and comfortable life.

This standard of well-being is manifest in the work of John H. Bodley (1975, 1977), an anthropologist who is among the most vocal opponents of development. On the surface Bodley seems to revive the

Boasian notion of relativism in attacking certain "ethnocentric mis-conceptions" about the disappearance of tribal peoples. For example, he argues against what he calls the "misconception" that tribal peoples reject their own cultures for a better way of life when civilization pre-sents itself (1975:5–9); he also argues against the "misconception" that our culture is superior (pp. 9–14). He writes:

> It is a virtual article of faith among cultural reformers that all people share our desire for what we define as material wealth, prosperity, and progress and that others have different cultures only because they have not yet been exposed to the superior technological alternatives offered by industrial civilizations. (p. 11)

Bodley argues that tribal peoples would prefer to be left alone and that they have accepted change primarily because they were forced to: as the industrial civilizations expanded throughout the world they gave others little choice but to accept "progress" (pp. 14–20).

Bodley goes farther in his argument that tribal peoples want to avoid change than most anthropologists would be comfortable with; surely he does not represent a sizable opinion within the discipline. What is significant about his argument, however, is that it is not based upon the Boasian principle of relativism at all, for it rests upon the very principle of material well-being that the Boasians rejected as a univer-sal standard. Bodley is saying that development schemes among non-industrial peoples are wrong because the changes such schemes incur worsen the peoples' material well-being, and do not improve it:

> In spite of the best intentions of those who have promoted change and improvement, all too often the real results have been poverty, longer working hours and much greater physical exertion, poor health, social disorder, discontent, discrimination, overpopulation, and environmental deterioration—all this combined with the destruction of the traditional culture. (p. 152)

We can now understand why ethical relativism has fallen on such hard times in spite of the resurgence of pessimism during the 1960s and later. First, it has been the experience of most anthropologists that non-Western peoples (and especially Third World nations) want change, at least to some extent; second, it is clear that they are often disadvantaged if it does not come; third, anthropologists by and large have altered their thinking about the relativity of material interests and improvement: most today consider these to be general values that can be applied throughout the world.

Not only has relativism fallen on hard times, it has become the subject of angry criticism, much of it from the Third World, which tends to conceive anthropologists as conservative in their attitudes toward change and therefore as promoting the subservience of the underdeveloped nations. For example, it seems that Third World anthropologists—those who are born and raised in Third World countries and then trained in anthropology in European or American universities—are often among the most severe critics of relativism today.*
An incident that happened to S. F. Nadel, a British anthropologist, is illustrative. In 1935, when he had just returned from his first field research in Nigeria, he was invited to speak at a meeting in London on "Anthropology and Colonial Government." His talk dealt with the role the anthropologist could play in the colonial system, and clearly Nadel's sympathies were with the native peoples. Yet when the talk was over, he commented, several West African students "violently attacked me, all my fellow workers in the field, and indeed the whole of anthropology." The students accused him and his colleagues "of playing into the hands of reactionary administrators and of lending the sanction of science to a policy meant to 'keep the African down' " (Nadel 1953:13). As Third World nations achieved independence after the war, the hostility they felt toward anthropology turned into official policy in many instances, and the discipline that imagined itself as the protector and benefactor of non-Western peoples now found itself *persona non grata* among them. For example, anthropologists of European and American background often found that their applications to enter these new nations for research were turned down (see Brokensha 1966:15–16).

* For example, see the comments following Lewis' article on "Anthropology and Colonialism" (Lewis 1973).

This hostility toward anthropology does not come exclusively from the belief that the discipline has helped to prevent change (see Lewis 1973). The discipline is also associated in people's minds with the earlier colonial rule and is often disliked (perhaps unfairly) on that basis alone; anthropologists are also accused of studying problems that are remote from the interests of the host nations, which want technical assistance in development, for example, and not esoteric analyses of the structure of descent groups or kinship systems. Field workers are criticized for advancing their personal careers at the expense of the people studied, for their writings usually appear in languages the people cannot read and are published in Western countries where the people cannot easily acquire them. What Third World nations want is research that will help them solve their problems, particularly problems of development, and they want the research to be published in a form they can use. So they see the anthropologist not only as a conservative force inhibiting change, but as someone who uses them as sources of information and who then does not provide a fair return.

The attack on the relativist's bias against change has also come from within the discipline, especially from radical anthropologists. Radical anthropology developed out of the political turmoil in the United States during the late 1960s, when the alienation of the left in this country was at its peak—as was its prime impetus and target, the Vietnam War. Radical anthropologists were never more than a minority of the discipline, yet they have been vocal and have had an important impact, particularly with their arguments about human exploitation. It is argued that anthropologists generally have ignored the existence of exploitation among the peoples they study; that this is one of the key dimensions to understand at all levels, from the local to the international; and that the anthropologist should not be neutral about it: he or she has the ethical responsibility to act in some way on behalf of the exploited. Radical anthropologists dispute the notion that colonialism is over, for even if independence has been won by Third World nations, the latter are still controlled by economic interests centering in Europe and North America. The key decisions affecting non-Western peoples today are made in the interest of profits for capitalist businesses (e.g., see Caulfield, in Hymes, ed. 1974:189–90).

The criticism that radical anthropologists make of ethical relativism is illustrated by one of the prominent works of the radical anthropology movement. This is the book *Reinventing Anthropology* (Hymes, ed., 1974), consisting of sixteen essays by as many writers who are either part of the movement or sympathetic to it. Discussions of relativism appear in a number of the essays, and in virtually every case the comments are negative. It is argued that relativism has turned the anthropologist's attention away from truly significant issues by fostering a preoccupation with pure, aboriginal patterns, those that are not contaminated by Western influence. Mina Caulfield refers to the value that relativists place on cultural differences as "romantic humanism"; she contends that the relativistic anthropologists "turned away from the social problems of the present and recent past," for they have preferred instead "to capture for humanity the vanishing puzzles and beauties of former cultures" (p. 184). Similarly, Dell Hymes notes that until very recently American Indians have been studied primarily to discover what their way of life was in the distant past, and not to find out what the people have become today (pp. 30–31). This turning away from the truly significant issues is due only in part to the humanistic appreciation for cultural differences, however, for it is also a result in part of the attempt to achieve an attitude of neutral detachment, or to remain value-free in research. Stanley Diamond remarks that "The result to which relativism logically tends, and which it never quite achieves, is to detach the anthropologist from all particular cultures. It does not provide him with a moral center, only a job; he can only strive to become a pure professional" (p. 422).

Whatever the cause, according to the radical critique, relativism has played directly into the hands of the oppressors throughout the world by its tacit support of the status quo. The relativists have not recognized that the exotic cultures to which they grant equal validity are poverty-stricken, powerless, and oppressed. William Willis comments that the relativist "avoids the distress and misery" of foreign peoples who are "cringing and cursing at the aggressive cruelty" of the Western nations (p. 126). This avoidance of the matter of oppression "helps explain the lack of outrage that has prevailed in anthropology until recent years." Willis writes: "Since relativism is applied only to 'aboriginal' customs, it advises colored peoples to preserve those customs that contributed to initial defeat and subsequent exploitation. . . . Hence, relativism defines the good life for colored peoples differently than for white people, and the good colored man is the man of the bush" (p. 144). Instead of leaving cultures as they are, as museum pieces, we should help to bring about change—or, better, we should help the oppressed to bring about change.

Some writers have also attempted to explain relativism, primarily the functionalist variety of British anthropology rather than the Boasian version, by reference to colonialism. Jacques Maquet has argued that (functionalist) relativism grew out of the colonial situation between the wars, and that in spite of anthropologists' good intentions, its actual effects were to buttress colonial rule by promoting a conservative posture: relativism bade us to proceed slowly with change and economic development, for otherwise we might upset the delicate, natural order of the native societies (1964:48–50). According to Maquet, there were progressive forces emerging in Africa and other colonial regions at the time, in that a growing number of tribal people were becoming educated in the European system and were now interested in change. Relativism worked against them. It also served to exclude the Africans from European society: by emphasizing the differences between Europeans and Africans, it set up a barrier that worked against the African who was interested in mobility (see also Asad, ed., 1973).

The view that anthropology should become more committed to change than it has been in the past is not unanimous by any means, but clearly it is widespread. By and large the disagreement among anthropologists has not been whether we should approve the relativist's call for cultural preservation (most say we should not) but why the status quo is undesirable. The view among radical anthropologists is primarily that the current state of affairs involves the exploitation of Third World peoples. To many who fall outside the radical camp, however, the status quo is undesirable because it perpetuates an undesirable level of material deprivation and suffering among those in the underdeveloped parts of the world.

In summary, immediately after World War II a number of forces

were at work against ethical relativism. The war posed a moral dilemma for the relativistic theory, the postwar sense of optimism stimulated a belief that it may be possible after all to arrive at general
moral principles, and the discipline itself was turning toward the search
for general theory and hence was amenable to the idea of moral absolutes. During the 1950s American anthropologists were writing not
as proponents of ethical relativism but as critics, for such people as
Linton, Kluckhohn, Redfield, and Kroeber were suggesting that anthropology can arrive at universal moral standards, and that human
history may even reveal a pattern of moral progress. Yet by the 1960s
this phase was clearly over, perhaps because the sense of optimism
turned. A growing cynicism became manifest in anthropologists' writings; for example, it now seemed out of the question that Western
civilization could point to itself as an example of moral progress. One
might think that the way was made for a return to relativism in the
1960s as the mood of pessimism grew, but this did not happen because
of a growing belief that the moral theory of tolerance contained a
crucial flaw. It tended to favor the status quo, which by now was
manifestly undesirable: by and large the Third World wants social,
political, and economic change, and is both disadvantaged and vulnerable if it does not come. What is more, anthropological thought
changed in a way that worked against a return to relativism, for the
view was growing that cultural interests are not as random as the pre-
World War II Boasians believed: increasingly it was felt that all people
share a similar orientation toward material comfort and welfare. Hence,
the status quo was now evaluated as undesirable because it entails the
material deprivation if not the exploitation of the Third World. The
current view now was that Western civilization may not be an unal-
loyed good, but that it has the moral obligation to help improve the
material conditions of non-Western peoples.

CHAPTER SEVEN

A Working Alternative

I F relativism is in such difficulty as a moral philosophy, is there any role at all left for it to play in our thinking? I believe so, and one of my purposes in this chapter is to indicate what that is. There is another purpose: given that much of ethical relativism has been nudged aside by recent events, I want to advance a set of principles that will cover much of the ground that relativism has relinquished. These principles constitute a framewock that we can use in evaluating cultures, including our own.

I will not try to give a satisfactory philosophical justification for the principles that follow. Such justification may be impossible to achieve, even by philosophers whose background in ethics is more secure than mine. This could lead some to conclude that the attempt to suggest general principles is misguided: would it not be better to accept a form of skepticism as a matter of necessity and to avoid cross-cultural value judgments? Yet skepticism here has moral consequences that are as unattractive as any that may follow from the principles I am about to suggest. If we hold that there truly are no valid principles that we may apply in assessing others, and that we should remain neutral in relation to them, then the tacit effect is to condone whatever takes place in foreign cultures. We are enjoined to look favorably on the brutalization of human beings by members of their own society, or upon the starvation of people whose subsistence system they themselves consider inadequate. Skepticism may be suitable for the philosopher who is interested in advancing the theoretical understanding of ethics, but in the context of interaction with foreign cultures, it is simply untenable. What follows is not to be taken as a contribution to the theoretical debate on normative ethics, a matter which would properly fall within the domain of philosophy. Rather, the purpose is to help clarify how we ought to react when we are confronted with behavior that is grounded in values different from our own, and also to help us define our own self-identity by indicating where we stand among human societies.

In saying that the following principles are not given full philosophical justification I do not mean that they have no justification at all, as will be evident as the discussion proceeds. These principles rest on a solid footing, in that a prima facie case can be made for them. Yet when a set of normative principles are accepted on prima facie grounds, deeper philosophical issues are left unresolved.

The first principle is that there is merit to the criticism that relativism has been accompanied by a conservative bias. What is at issue here is the relativist claim that all cultures or institutions are equally valid or fitting: anthropologists tended to assume that the mere presence of a cultural trait warrants our valuing it. Elizabeth Colson has put the case quite simply; she wrote, "Ethnographers have usually presented each social group they study as a success story. We have no reason to believe that this is true" (1976:264). A people may get by with inadequate solutions to their problems even judging by their own standards. For example, if the people are genuinely interested in ensuring the productivity of their gardens, they will find innovations like crop rotation and fertilization more effective than human sacrifice—although they will not have the statistical evidence to realize this (cf. Bagish 1981:12–20).

Second, a general principle is at hand for judging the adequacy of institutions. It may be called the humanistic principle or standard, by which I mean that the well-being of people ought to be respected. The notion of well-being is a critical aspect of the humanistic principle, and three points can be made with respect to it. For one, I assume that human well-being is not a culture-bound idea. Starvation and violence, for example, are hardly products of Western thought or a function of Western thinking, although they may be conceived in a peculiarly Western idiom. Starvation and violence are phenomena that are recognized as such in the most diverse cultural traditions. Another is that the notion of human well-being is inherently value-laden, and concepts of harm and beneficence are inseparable from it: it seems impossible to imagine the idea of human well-being divorced from moral judgments of approval and disapproval. Whereas such notions as sky or earth may conceivably be held in purely neutral terms in a given culture, such ideas as hunger and torture cannot be. It is even reasonable to argue that the *point* of morality, as a philosophical if not a sociological issue, is to promote the well-being of others (Warnock 1971, esp. pp. 12–26). Finally, the notion of human well-being, when used as the central point of morality, serves to root moral questions in the physical, emotional, and intellectual constitution of people. It may be that any rigorous attempt to work out the content of morality will have to include an analysis of such notions as human wants, needs, interests, and happiness.

The humanistic principle can be divided into two parts. First is Redfield's point about humaneness, that it is good to treat people well, or that we should not do one another harm. We can judge that human sacrifice, torture, and political repression are wrong, whether they occur in our society or some other. Similarly, it is wrong for a person, whatever society he or she may belong to, to be indifferent toward the suffering of others. The matter of coercion, discussed earlier, fits here, in that we may judge it to be wrong when some members of a society deliberately and forcefully interfere in the affairs of other people. Coercion works against the well-being of those toward whom it is directed. Second is the notion that people ought to enjoy a reasonable level of material existence: we may judge that poverty, malnutrition, material discomfort, human suffering, and the like are bad. These two ideas may be brought together to form one standard since both concern the physical well-being of the members of society, and the difference between them is that the former refers to the quality of interpersonal relations, and the latter to the material conditions under which people live.

The humanistic principle may be impossible to define very tightly; it may even be that the best we can do to give it shape is to illustrate it with examples as I have done here. And surely it is difficult to apply in actual situations. Yet these are not good reasons to avoid making judgments about the relative merit of institutions or about the desirability of change. Although we may do harm by expressing judgments across cultural boundaries, we may do as much or more harm by failing to do so.

The orthodox relativist would perhaps argue that there is no humanistic moral principle that we can use for this purpose, in that notions like harm and discomfort are quite variable from one culture to the next. Pain and personal injury may even be highly valued by some people. For example, the Plains Indian willingly engaged in a form of self-torture that a middle-class American could hardly tolerate. The Indians chopped off finger joints and had arrows skewered through their flesh; tied to the arrows were cords, by which the sufferer dragged buffalo skulls around the village. Some American Indians were also reported to have placed a very high value on bravery, and the captive who withstood torture without showing pain was highly regarded by the enemies who tormented him.

Yet cases like these do not make the point that notions of pain and suffering are widely variable. Following this same logic one could say that middle-class Americans value pain since they willingly consent to surgery, and the man or woman who bears up well is complimented for his or her strength of character. The Indian who was tortured to death would surely have preferred a long and respectable life among his people to the honorable death that came to him. The Plains Indian who engaged in self-torture was trying to induce a vision (in our idiom, a hallucination) for the power and advantages it was believed such an experience would bring. The pain was a means to an end, and surely was not seen as a pleasurable indulgence to look forward to. The difference between middle-class Americans and Plains Indians on this point could be a difference in judgments of reality and not a difference in values—the American would not believe that the vision has the significance attributed to it by the Indian, so he or she would not submit to the pain. Similarly, the Plains warrior might not believe in the efficacy of surgery and might refuse to suffer the scalpel.

The widespread trend among non-Western peoples to want such material benefits as steel knives and other labor-saving devices is a clear indication that all is not relative when it comes to hard work, hunger, discomfort, and the like. Cultural values may be widely different in many ways, but in this sphere at least, human beings do seem to have certain preferences in common.

The Yanomamö are an instructive case, for here is a people who do not seem to share the humanistic value I am suggesting. The level of violence and treachery in this society suggests that their regard for pain and suffering is demonstrably different from what I am arguing is the norm among human beings. Yet this is not clearly the case either: individuals in Yanomamö society are more willing than middle-class Americans to inflict injury on others, yet they want to avoid injury to themselves. Why else would the wife flee in terror when her husband comes at her with a machete, and why else would a village seek refuge from enemies when it is outnumbered and weak? The Yanomamö seem rather to be a case in which we are warranted in making a value judgment across cultural boundaries: they do not exhibit as much regard for the well-being of other persons as they have for themselves, and this can be judged a moral error.

Does this point about the generality of the humanistic principle among human beings not make the same mistake that Herskovits, Benedict, and other relativists were accused of making, which is to derive an "ought" from an "is"? My argument is not quite that simple, for it has two parts. First is the generalization that the humanistic value seems to be widespread among human beings. Second, I am making the moral judgment (quite separately from the empirical generalization) that this is an estimable value to hold, or that it warrants acceptance—in contrast, say, to another widespread value, ethnocentrism, which is not meritorious even if it is universal.

A third principle in the scheme that I propose is that a considerable portion of the cultural inventory of a people falls outside the scope of the humanistic standard mentioned above. In other words, once we have considered those cultural features that we can reasonably judge by this standard, a large portion remains, and it consists of those items which have little if anything to do with the strictly practical affairs of life and which then cannot be appraised by practical considerations. Included are sexual mores, marriage patterns, kinship relations, styles of leadership, forms of etiquette, attitudes toward work and personal advancement, dietary preferences, clothing styles, conceptions of deity, and others. Some of these nonappraisable features are closely linked to others that are, in that there are always nonessential cultural accouterments or trappings associated with institutions that are important on practical grounds. Western medicine provides a surfeit of examples. Health care clearly falls within the orbit of the humanistic principle, yet much of the medical system in the United States is hardly necessary for health's sake, including the rigid social hierarchy among doctors and nurses and the traditional division of labor between them. Successful health care systems can assume different forms from the one exhibited in this country. It is essential (but difficult) to keep in mind this division between what is essential and what is not in such matters as medicine, for otherwise civilization will tend to pack a good deal of unnecessary cultural baggage along with the genuinely useful features when it sets out to share its advantages with others.

Relativism prevails in relation to the institutions that fall outside the orbit of the humanistic principle, for here a genuine diversity of values is found and there are no suitable cross-cultural standards for evaluating them. The finest reasoning that we or anyone else can achieve will not point decisively to the superiority of Western marriage patterns, eating habits, legal institutions, and the like. We ought to show tolerance with respect to these institutions in other societies on the grounds that people ought to be free to live as they choose.

This leads to the fourth principle: is it possible to identify any areas of culture in which we may speak of improvement? Are there any criteria that will produce a hierarchical ordering of societies that we may say represents a pattern of advance? Or is the distinction between primitive and civilized societies but an expression of our cultural bias?

The first criterion that comes to mind is Redfield's and Kroeber's, according to which civilization has brought a more humane existence, a higher level of morality to mankind, inasmuch as people treat one another better in complex societies. This judgment is very difficult to accept today, however. Recent events have left most of us with considerable ambivalence about Western democracy, to cite one instance. Politicians seem too often to be both incompetent and dishonest, and to be willing to allow private economic interests to influence programs

and policies at all levels. Similarly, there is a very strong distrust of
the power and intentions of big business, which seems to set its policies chiefly by looking at its margin of profit. The risk of producing a
dangerous product is calculated by assessing how much the company
is liable to lose in lawsuits relative to its profits, and not by considering
the real dangers to human life. Much of the difficulty of assessing
moral advance is that this is a highly impressionistic matter. The ledger
sheets on which we tote up the pluses and minuses for each culture
are so complex that summary calculations of overall moral standing
are nearly meaningless. Perhaps the most one can say about whether
or not there has been moral advance is that it is impossible to tell—
but that it is not very likely.

It is important to distinguish between this conclusion and Herskovits'. According to him, we cannot speak of progress in this sphere
because any humanistic principle we might use will necessarily be
culture-bound; we have no yardstick to measure with. My point is that
we do have a suitable yardstick, but that there are so many measures to
take in each culture that the sum total is too complicated to assess.

Another criterion for gauging improvement is the material well-being
of people: disregarding whether or not the members of society behave
well or ill toward one another, can we say that the material conditions
of life have gotten better with civilization? In pursuing this question I
need to digress somewhat. The issue of material improvement places
the focus on economics and technology, and also on such technical
knowledge as that which is provided by medical and agricultural research. So we need first to ask if it is possible to arrive at an objective
and meaningful hierarchy of societies based on these features. Herskovits questioned that we can. To him, an ordering of societies according to our criterion of economic production and technological
complexity will merely reflect our cultural perspective and not some
fundamental principle of general significance to all peoples.

Herskovits' argument is off the mark. On one hand, the criterion of
economic complexity and technological sophistication is objective in
the sense that it is definable by reference to empirical features that are
independent of our culture. For example, the intensity and scale of
economic transactions have a physical aspect which is identifiable from

other cultural perspectives than ours, and the same is true of such measures as the amount of food produced per farm worker.* What is more, the social hierarchy that results from the use of these criteria has historical significance: one would be astonished, say, to discover evidence of complex forms of agricultural production in the Paleolithic. But on the other hand, and even more important, this is a meaningful hierarchy, in that the point of this ordering of societies would not be lost on people from other cultures; it would be meaningful to them because they see the value of increasing agricultural productivity, the use of bicycles (and automobiles), the availability of running water, and the like. It is surely the case that non-Western peoples all over the world are more interested in the products of Western industrial production than they are in the intricacies of Australian kinship, and are more likely to incorporate such Western innovations as fertilizers and matches into their cultures than they are the particulars of the Australian system of marriage and descent. This is an important message we get from the post-World War II drive for economic development among the newly independent nations.

There is a danger in using people's perceptions of the relative superiority of economic and technological systems as a test for the meaningfulness of this social hierarchy, because not all of the world's populations agree about what it is that is good about development and modernization. For example, Burma and Iran are highly selective in the changes they will accept, and at least some very simple societies (like the Andaman Islanders) want little if any change.

There is another way to establish the hierarchy without relying completely and directly on people's opinions. However another society may feel about what they do or do not want with regard to development, the economic and technological relationship between them and Western societies is asymmetrical. It is true that the fully developed nations rely on the less developed ones for natural resources like oil, but processed goods, and both economic and technological innova-

---

* The World Bank and other organizations commonly use a number of objective measures in assessing such matters as poverty, physical quality of life, and economic and social development. For example, see Lizer 1977, and World Bank 1979:117–188.

tions, flow chiefly to and not away from the societies that are lower
on the scale. To take an extreme case, there is little in the sphere of
technology and economics that the Australian aborigines or Andaman
Islanders can offer to the developed nations, whereas the reverse is not
true. For example, some of the most isolated Andaman Islanders occasionally find empty gasoline drums washed upon their shore. They
cut these in half and use them as enormous cooking pots (Cipriani
1966:52). It is unthinkable that this relationship could be reversed—
that we would find some technological item from their cultural inventory to be especially useful in our everyday lives. It is true that we may
value their pottery or other artifacts as examples of primitive art, but
the use we have for such items is esthetic, not practical, and consequently such items are of a different order from the gasoline drums
that the Andamanese find so useful.

In noting this asymmetry I do not mean that cultures which are
lower in the hierarchy do not have a very sophisticated technical
knowledge of their own (they must in order to survive) and in this
sense "they have something to teach us," as Brokensha and Riley re-
mark concerning the Mbeere of Kenya. "In fact," these writers continue, "Mbeere and other folk-belief systems contain much that is based
on extremely accurate, detailed and thoughtful observations, made over
many generations" (1980:115). It is easy to depreciate or ignore the
cultural practices and ideas of another society, say, when assisting them
in the process of development. In particular, it is tempting to want to
replace their traditional practices with "modern" ones in wholesale
fashion, instead of building on or incorporating the indigenous knowledge in helping to bring about change. Nevertheless, the presence of
such useful knowledge in indigenous systems of thought does not negate the fundamental asymmetry that exists among societies or the
hierarchy which the asymmetry suggests.

The pluralistic notion of development mentioned in chapter 6 has
bearing on the way we should conceive this hierarchy. The idea that
Third World countries should become more and more like Western
industrial societies is subject to criticism, and it may be preferable to
define development differently for each society according to the interests of the people concerned and the nature of their economic and

ecological conditions. A people may have achieved as much development as they need and want without embarking on a trajectory of
industrial "growth" in the Western sense. In other words, the hierarchy I am suggesting does not represent a set of stages through which
all societies will necessarily want to pass. It is simply a ranking of
cultural systems according to degrees of economic complexity, technological sophistication, and the like.

Yet this begs a crucial question. Is it not true that to suggest this
hierarchy is to imply that the societies higher on the scale are preferable? Does the existence of the hierarchy not mean that the societies
that fall below would be better off if only they could manage to come
up to a higher level of economic complexity and technological sophistication?

The discussion now comes back to the issue that prompted this
digression. Can we say that the social hierarchy we have arrived at
represents improvement or advance? The response unfortunately is as
indecisive as the one concerning moral progress, and for the same
reason. On one hand, civilization has brought a lower infant mortality
rate due to better diet, hygiene, and medical care; less vulnerability to
infectious disease for the same reasons; greater economic security due
to increased economic diversification; less danger from local famine
due to improved systems of transportation and economic organization;
greater material comfort due to improved housing, and the like. But
on the other hand we have pollution, the horrors of modern warfare,
and the boredom and alienation of factory work, to name a few. On
one hand we have labor-saving devices like automatic dishwashers, but
on the other we have to spend our lives on a treadmill to pay for them.
The tally sheet is simply too complicated to make an overall judgment. It is not at all clear that other people should want to become
like Western civilization.

What we can say about the hierarchy is that the nations that fall
toward the upper end of the scale have greater resources than the others. They have better technical knowledge from which the entire world
may benefit—knowledge about hygiene, diet, crop rotation, soils, and
the like. They also have the physical capacity to undertake programs
of assistance when other societies are interested. Yet the higher civili-

zations also have the capacity to do far greater harm. The industrial system has exploited the powerless, ravaged the environment, meddled in the affairs of other countries, and conducted war in ways that the simpler societies never dreamed of. Even when we set out altruistically to help others we often mismanage the effort or misunderstand what it is we should do. Just as it is not at all clear that industrial civilization provides a happier or more fulfilling life for its members, so it is not clear whether its overall influence on those below it in the hierarchy has been to their detriment or benefit. This is a pessimistic age, and at this point it is difficult to suppress a strong sense of despair on this score.

The place of Western civilization in the hierarchy of human societies is very different from what it was thought to be by Victorian anthropologists, who saw the differences among societies at bottom as a matter of intelligence: civilization is more thoughtful and shows greater sense than the lower societies, and it provides a happier and more benign mode of living; savages would embrace our way of life if they had the intelligence to understand it, for their institutions are but imperfect specimens of our own. Clearly this is inadequate. Many areas of life cannot be judged by standards that apply across cultural boundaries, for in many respects cultures are oriented in widely different directions. Still, all people desire material comfort and security, and in this sense Western civilization is distinguished from other cultures. The relationship among societies in this respect is one of asymmetry. Just as we may do far more harm to others than they can do to us, so we may do them more good, and we have the obligation to share the material advantages our civilization has to offer. Yet this asymmetry should not be confused with superiority. As a total way of life ours may not be preferable to others, and we need not try to turn them into copies of Western civilization.

An important implication follows from these conclusions: it is possible to arrive at a general principle for evaluating institutions without assuming that ours is a superior way of life. Herskovits for one seems to have believed that this could not be done, and that any general moral principle we might advance would express our own cultural bias and would tacitly make us appear to occupy a position superior to the rest. But this is not so. The matter of arriving at general moral principles and of how we measure up to these principles are two very separate issues.

The idea of ethical relativism in anthropology has had a complicated history. Through the 1930s the discipline expressed an overwhelming confidence in the notion, a confidence that was fortified by the empirical findings about the variability of moral values from culture to culture. And relativism was thought to be an idea of signal importance, for it could be used in world affairs and would contribute to peace and human understanding. But suddenly and with firm conviction, relativism was swept aside. It had all been a mistake.

Was relativism completely mistaken? After we have excised what is unacceptable, is there something left, a residuum of some kind, that still warrants approval? Certainly the relativists' call for tolerance contained an element that is hard to fault. This is the value of freedom: people ought to be free to live as they choose, to be free from the coercion of others more powerful than they. Equally fundamental, perhaps, is the message that relativism contained about the place of Western civilization among human societies. Rejected was the smug belief in Western superiority that dominated anthropological thinking during the 1800s. Just as the universe has not looked the same since the Copernican revolution, so the world and our place in it has not looked the same since ethical relativism appeared at about the turn of this century.

Bibliography

Agassiz, Louis. 1866. *The Structure of Animal Life.* New York: Scribners.

Andreski, Stanislav. 1972. *Social Sciences as Sorcery.* London: Deutsch.

Arensberg, Conrad M. and Arthur H. Niehoff. 1971. *Introducing Social Change: A Manual for Community Development.* Chicago and New York: Aldine.

Asad, Talal, ed. 1973. *Anthropology and the Colonial Encounter.* Atlantic Highlands, N.J.: Humanities Press.

Bagish, Henry H. 1981. *Confessions of a Former Cultural Relativist.* (Second Annual Faculty Lecture, Santa Barbara City College, 1981.) Santa Barbara: Santa Barbara City College Publications.

Beard, Charles A. 1913. *An Economic Interpretation of the Constitution of the United States.* New York: Macmillan.

Beattie, John. 1964. *Other Cultures: Aims, Methods and Achievements in Social Anthropology.* New York: Free Press.

Benedict, Ruth. 1934a. *Patterns of Culture.* Boston: Houghton Mifflin.

—— 1934b. "Anthropology and the Abnormal." *Journal of General Psychology* 10:59–82.

Bidney, David. 1968. "Cultural Relativism." In David L. Sills, ed., *International Encyclopedia of the Social Sciences.* New York: Macmillan and Free Press.

Bieder, Robert. 1972. "The American Indian and the Development of Anthropological Thought in the United States, 1780–1851." Ph.D. dissertation, University of Minnesota.

Boas, Franz. 1894. "Human Faculty as Determined by Race." *Proceedings of the American Association for the Advancement of Science* 43:301–27.

—— 1901. "The Mind of Primitive Man." *Journal of American Folk-Lore* 14:1–11.

—— 1904. "The History of Anthropology." *Science*. N.S., 20:513–24.

—— 1908. *Anthropology*. New York: Columbia University Press.

—— 1938. *The Mind of Primitive Man*. Revised edition. New York: Free Press (1965 edition).

—— 1966. *Race, Language, and Culture*. New York: Free Press.

Bodley, John H. 1975. *Victims of Progress*. Menlo Park, Calif.: Cummings.

—— 1977. "Alternatives to Ethnocide: Human Zoos, Living Museums, and Real People." In Elias Sevilla-Casas, ed., *Western Expansion and Indigenous Peoples: The Heritage of Las Casas*. The Hague: Mouton.

Brandt, Richard B. 1954. *Hopi Ethics: A Theoretical Analysis*. Chicago: University of Chicago Press.

—— 1959. *Ethical Theory*. Englewood Cliffs, N.J.: Prentice-Hall.

—— 1967. "Ethical Relativism." In Paul Edwards, ed., *The Encyclopedia of Philosophy*. New York: Macmillan and Free Press.

Brinton, Crane. 1950. *Ideas and Men: The Story of Western Thought*. New York: Prentice-Hall.

British Broadcasting Corporation. 1949. *Ideas and Beliefs of the Victorians*. New York: Dutton (1966 edition).

Brokensha, David. 1966. *Applied Anthropology in English-Speaking Africa*. Society for Applied Anthropology, Monograph No. 8.

Brokensha, David, and Bernard W. Riley. 1980. "Mbeere Knowledge of Their Vegetation, and its Relevance for Development (Kenya)." In David Brokensha, D. M. Warren, and Oswald Werner, eds., *Indigenous Knowledge Systems and Development*. Lanham, Md.: University Press of America.

Burrow, J. W. 1966. *Evolution and Society: A Study in Victorian Social Theory*. London: Cambridge University Press.

Carneiro, Robert. 1968. "Spencer, Herbert." In David L. Sills, ed., *International Encyclopedia of the Social Sciences*. New York: Macmillan and Free Press.

Chagnon, Napoleon A. 1977. *Yanomamö: The Fierce People*. 2d ed. New York: Holt, Rinehart and Winston.

Cipriani, Lidio. 1966. *The Andaman Islanders.* Edited and translated by D. Tayler Cox. New York: Praeger.

Cole, Michael and Sylvia Scribner. 1974. *Culture and Thought.* New York: Wiley.

Colson, Elizabeth. 1976. "Culture and Progress." *American Anthropologist* 78:261–71.

Commager, Henry Steele. 1950. *The American Mind: An Interpretation of American Thought and Character Since the 1880s.* New Haven: Yale University Press.

Cook, John. 1978. "Cultural Relativism as an Ethnocentric Notion." In Roger Beehler and Alan R. Drengson, eds., *The Philosophy of Society.* London: Methuen.

Dalton, George. 1971. "Introduction." In George Dalton, ed., *Economic Development and Social Change.* Garden City, N.Y.: Natural History Press.

Darnell, Regna. 1969. "The Development of American Anthropology, 1880–1920: From the Bureau of American Ethnology to Franz Boas." Ph.D. dissertation, University of Pennsylvania.

—— 1976. "Daniel Brinton and the Professionalization of American Anthropology." In John V. Murra, ed., *American Anthropology: The Early Years.* St. Paul: West.

Davis, Kingsley and Wilbert E. Moore. 1945. "Some Principles of Stratification." *American Sociological Review* 10:242–49.

Duncker, Karl. 1939. "Ethical Relativity? (An Inquiry Into the Psychology of Ethics)." *Mind* 48:39–53.

Edel, Abraham. 1955. *Ethical Judgment: The Use of Science in Ethics.* Glencoe, Ill.: The Free Press.

Edel, May and Abraham Edel. 1959. *Anthropology and Ethics.* Springfield, Ill.: Charles C. Thomas.

Eiseley, Loren. 1961. *Darwin's Century: Evolution and the Men Who Discovered It.* Garden City, N.Y.: Anchor Books.

Emmet, Dorothy. 1968. "Ethical Systems and Social Structures." In David L. Sills, ed., *International Encyclopedia of the Social Sciences.* New York: Macmillan and Free Press.

Erasmus, Charles J. 1967. "Obviating the Functions of Functionalism." *Social Forces* 45:319–28.

Feinberg, Joel. 1973. *Social Philosophy*. Englewood Cliffs, N.J.: Prentice-Hall.

Foot, Philippa. 1979. *Moral Relativism*. Lindley Lecture, University of Kansas, 1978. Lawrence: University of Kansas Press.

Frankena, William K. 1973. *Ethics*. 2d ed. Englewood Cliffs, N.J.: Prentice-Hall.

Fried, Morton H. 1967. *The Evolution of Political Society: An Essay in Political Anthropology*. New York: Random House.

Ginsberg, Morris. 1953. "On the Diversity of Morals." *Journal of the Royal Anthropological Institute* 83:117–35.

Goldenweiser, Alexander. 1922. *Ancient Civilization: An Introduction to Anthropology*. New York: Knopf.

Graham, Otis L., Jr. 1971. *The Great Campaigns: Reform and War in America, 1900–1928*. Englewood Cliffs, N.J.: Prentice-Hall.

Greene, John C. 1961. *The Death of Adam: Evolution and Its Impact on Western Thought*. New York: Mentor Books.

Gregg, Dorothy and Elgin Williams. 1948. "The Dismal Science of Functionalism." *American Anthropologist* 50:594–611.

Gruber, Jacob W. 1965. "Brixham Cave and the Antiquity of Man." In Melford E. Spiro, ed., *Context and Meaning in Cultural Anthropology*. New York: Free Press.

—— 1967. "Horatio Hale and the Development of American Anthropology." *Proceedings of the American Philosophical Society* 3:5–37.

Hallowell, A. Irving. 1960. "The Beginnings of Anthropology in America." In Frederica de Laguna, ed., *Selected Papers from the American Anthropologist, 1888–1920*. Evanston and Elmsford: Row, Peterson.

Hanson, F. Allan. 1975. *Meaning in Culture*. London and Boston: Routledge and Kegan Paul.

Harris, Marvin. 1960. "Adaptation in Biological and Cultural Science." *Transactions of the New York Academy of Sciences*. Ser. 2, 23: 59–65.

—— 1968. *The Rise of Anthropological Theory*. New York: Crowell.

—— 1971. *Culture, Man, and Nature: An Introduction to Cultural Anthropology*. New York: Crowell.

—— 1974. *Cows, Pigs, Wars and Witches: The Riddles of Culture*. New York: Random House.

—— 1977. *Cannibals and Kings: The Origins of Cultures*. New York: Random House.

Hartung, Frank. 1954. "Cultural Relativity and Moral Judgments." *Philosophy of Science* 21:118–26.

Hatch, Elvin. 1973a. *Theories of Man and Culture*. New York: Columbia University Press.

—— 1973b. "The Growth of Economic, Subsistence, and Ecological Studies in American Anthropology." *Journal of Anthropological Research* 29:221–43.

Helm, June. 1966. *Pioneers of American Anthropology: The Uses of Biography*. Seattle: University of Washington Press.

Herskovits, Melville J. 1947. *Man and His Works*. New York: Knopf.

—— 1973. *Cultural Relativism: Perspectives in Cultural Pluralism*. New York: Vintage Books.

Hill, Helen. 1975. " 'Peripheral Capitalism,' Beyond 'Dependency' and 'Modernisation.' " *The Australian and New Zealand Journal of Sociology* 11:30–37.

Hinsley, Curtis M., Jr. 1976. "Amateurs and Professionals in Washington Anthropology, 1879 to 1903." In John V. Murra, ed., *American Anthropology: The Early Years*. St. Paul: West.

Hofstadter, Richard. 1955. *The Age of Reform: From Bryan to F.D.R.* New York: Vintage Books.

Hogbin, H. Ian. 1951. *Transformation Scene: The Changing Culture of a New Guinea Village*. London: Routledge and Kegan Paul.

—— 1958. *Social Change*. London: Watts.

Honigmann, John J. 1976. *The Development of Anthropological Ideas*. Homewood, Ill.: Dorsey Press.

Hughes, H. Stuart. 1958. *Consciousness and Society: The Reorientation of European Social Thought, 1890–1930*. New York: Vintage Books.

Hymes, Dell, ed. 1974. *Reinventing Anthropology*. New York: Vintage Books.

Jarvie, I. C. 1970. "Understanding and Explanation in Sociology and Social Anthropology." In Robert Borger and Frank Cioffi, eds., *Explanation in the Behavioral Sciences*. Cambridge: Cambridge University Press.

—— 1973. *Functionalism*. Minneapolis: Burgess.

Judd, Neil M. 1967. *The Bureau of American Ethnology, A Partial History*. Norman: University of Oklahoma Press.

Kaplan, David and Robert A. Manners. 1972. *Culture Theory*. Englewood Cliffs, N.J.: Prentice-Hall.

Kennedy, Raymond. 1943. "Acculturation and Administration in Indonesia." *American Anthropologist* 45:185–92.

Kluckhohn, Clyde. 1939. "The Place of Theory in Anthropological Studies." *The Philosophy of Science* 6:328–44.

—— 1949. *Mirror for Man*. New York and Toronto: McGraw-Hill.

—— 1953. "Universal Categories of Culture." In A. L. Kroeber, ed., *Anthropology Today*. Chicago: University of Chicago Press.

—— 1955. "Ethical Relativity: *Sic et Non*." *Journal of Philosophy* 52:663–77.

Kroeber, A. L. 1917. "The Superorganic." *American Anthropologist* 19:163–213.

—— 1948. *Anthropology*. Rev. ed. New York: Harcourt Brace.

—— 1952. *The Nature of Culture*. Chicago: University of Chicago Press.

Ladd, John. 1957. *The Structure of a Moral Code: A Philosophical Analysis of Ethical Discourse Applied to the Ethics of the Navaho Indians*. Cambridge: Harvard University Press.

—— 1973. *Ethical Relativism*. Belmont, Calif.: Wadsworth.

de Laguna, Grace A. 1942. "Cultural Relativism and Science." *The Philosophical Review* 51:141–66.

Lewis, Diane. 1973. "Anthropology and Colonialism." *Current Anthropology* 14:581–602.

Linton, Ralph. 1936. *The Study of Man*. New York: Appleton-Century-Crofts.

—— 1952. "Universal Ethical Principles: An Anthropological View."

In Ruth Nanda Anshen, ed., *Moral Principles of Action: Man's Ethical Imperative*. New York and London: Harper.

—— 1954. "The Problem of Universal Values." In Robert F. Spencer, ed., *Method and Perspective in Anthropology*. Minneapolis: University of Minnesota Press.

Lizer, Florizelle B. 1977. "Statistical Annexes." In John H. Sewell, *The United States and World Development, Agenda, 1977*. New York: Praeger.

Lovejoy, Arthur O. 1936. *The Great Chain of Being: A Study of the History of an Idea*. New York: Harper and Row.

Lowie, Robert H. 1917. *Culture and Ethnology*. New York: Basic Books (1966 edition).

—— 1920. *Primitive Society*. New York: Harper Torchbook (1961 edition).

—— 1929. *Are We Civilized? Human Culture in Perspective*. New York: Harcourt, Brace.

MacBeath, Alexander. 1952. *Experiments in Living: A Study of the Nature and Foundation of Ethics or Morals in the Light of Recent Work in Social Anthropology*. London: Macmillan.

Mair, Lucy. 1965. "Tradition and Modernity in the New Africa." *Transactions of the New York Academy of Sciences*, Series 2, 27:439–44.

Malinowski, Bronislaw. 1948. *Magic Science, and Religion and Other Essays*. Garden City, N.Y.: Anchor Books.

Maquet, Jaques J. 1964. "Objectivity in Anthropology." *Current Anthropology* 5:47–55.

Marnham, Patrick. 1977. *Nomads of the Sahel*. London: Minority Rights Group, Report No. 33.

May, Henry F. 1959. *The End of American Innocence: A Study of the First Years of Our Time, 1912–1917*. New York: Knopf.

Mead, Margaret. 1956. *New Lives for Old*. New York: William Morrow.

Morgan, Lewis Henry. 1877. *Ancient Society*. Edited with an introduction and annotations by Eleanor Burke Leacock. Cleveland and New York: Meridian Books (1963 ed.).

Moser, Shia. 1968. *Absolutism and Relativism in Ethics*. Springfield, Ill., Charles C. Thomas.

MRG. 1974. *The Montagnards of South Vietnam*. London: Minority Rights Group, Report No. 18.

Murdock, George Peter. 1965. *Culture and Society*. Pittsburgh: University of Pittsburgh Press.

Murphree, Idus L. 1961. "The Evolutionary Anthropologists: The Progress of Mankind. The Concepts of Progress and Culture in the Thought of John Lubbock, Edward B. Tylor, and Lewis H. Morgan." *Proceedings of the American Philosophical Society* 105:265–300.

Nadel, S. F. 1953. *Anthropology and Modern Life*. Canberra: Australian National University.

Needham, Rodney. 1972. *Belief, Language, and Experience*. Chicago: University of Chicago Press.

Phillips, D. Z. and H. O. Mounce. 1970. *Moral Practices*. New York: Schocken Books.

Pollard, Sidney. 1968. *The Idea of Progress*. Harmondsworth, Middlesex: Penguin Books (1971 ed.).

Radcliffe-Brown, A. R. 1952. *Structure and Function in Primitive Society*. Glencoe: Free Press.

—— 1958. *Method in Social Anthropology*. Chicago: University of Chicago Press.

Redfield, Robert. 1953. *The Primitive World and Its Transformations*. Ithaca: Cornell University Press (1957 ed.).

—— 1957. "The Universally Human and Culturally Variable." *Journal of General Education* 10:150–60.

Rudolph, Wolfgang. 1968. *Der Kulturelle Relativismus: Kritische Analyse einer Grundsatzfragen-Diskussion in der Amerikanischen Ethnologie*. Berlin: Duncker and Humblot.

Russell, Bertrand. 1945. *A History of Western Philosophy*. New York: Simon & Schuster.

Sahlins, Marshall D. 1960. "Evolution: Specific and General." In Marshall D. Sahlins and Elman R. Service, eds., *Evolution and Culture*. Ann Arbor: University of Michigan Press.

—— 1977. *Culture and Practical Reason.* Chicago: University of Chicago Press.

Schmidt, Paul H. 1955. "Some Criticisms of Cultural Relativism." *Journal of Philosophy* 52:780–91.

Service, Elman R. 1971. *Primitive Social Organization: An Evolutionary Perspective.* 2d ed. New York: Random House.

Spencer, Herbert. 1857. "Progress: Its Law and Cause." Reprinted in *Essays, Scientific, Political, and Speculative.* New York: Appleton (1904 ed.).

—— 1897. *The Principles of Sociology.* New York: Appleton.

Stace, W. T. 1962. *The Concept of Morals.* New York: Macmillan.

Stocking, George W., Jr. 1968a. *Race, Culture, and Evolution: Essays in the History of Anthropology.* New York: Free Press.

—— 1968b. "Tylor, Edward Burnett." In David L. Sills, ed., *International Encyclopedia of the Social Sciences.* New York: Macmillan and Free Press.

—— 1971. "What's In a Name? The Origins of the Royal Anthropological Institute (1837–71)." *Man* 6:369–90.

—— 1973. "From Chronology to Ethnology: James Cowles Prichard and British Anthropology 1800–1850." In George W. Stocking, Jr., ed., *Researches into the Physical History of Man,* by James Cowles Prichard. Chicago: University of Chicago Press.

—— 1974. *The Shaping of American Anthropology, 1883–1911: A Franz Boas Reader.* New York: Basic Books.

—— 1976. "Ideas and Institutions in American Anthropology: Thoughts Toward a History of the Interwar Years." In George W. Stocking, Jr., ed., *Selected Papers from the American Anthropologist, 1921–1949.* Washington, D.C.: American Anthropological Association.

Sumner, William Graham. 1906. *Folkways.* Boston: Athenaeum Press.

Taylor, Paul W. 1958. "Social Science and Ethical Relativism." *Journal of Philosophy* 55:32–44.

Tennekes, J. 1971. *Anthropology, Relativism, and Method: An Inquiry into the Methodological Principles of a Science of Culture.* Assen: Koninklijke Van Gorcum.

Thoresen, Timothy H. H., ed. 1975. *Toward a Science of Man: Essays in the History of Anthropology*. The Hague: Mouton.

Torgerson, Dial. 1981. "Tiny Group Rescues Pregnant Arab Girls." *Los Angeles Times*, January 4, 1981, part 1, p. 1.

Tumin, Melvin M. 1953. "Some Principles of Stratification: A Critical Analysis." *American Sociological Review* 18:387–94.

Tylor, Edward B. 1971. *Primitive Culture*. 2 vols. New York: Harper Torchbooks (1958 ed.).

—— 1881. *Anthropology: An Introduction to the Study of Man*. New York: Appleton (1898 ed.).

Veblen, Thorstein. 1899. *The Theory of the Leisure Class*. Boston: Houghton Mifflin.

Voget, Fred W. 1975. *A History of Ethnology*. New York: Holt, Rinehart, and Winston.

von Fritz, Kurt. 1952. "Relative and Absolute Values." In Ruth Nanda Anshen, ed., *Moral Principles of Action: Man's Ethical Imperative*. New York and London: Harpers.

de Waal Malefijt, Annemarie. 1974. *Images of Man: A History of Anthropological Thought*. New York: Knopf.

Wagar, W. Warren. 1972. *Good Tidings: The Belief in Progress from Darwin to Marcuse*. Bloomington: Indiana University Press.

Warnock, G. J. 1971. *The Object of Morality*. London: Methuen.

Westermarck, Edward A. 1932. *Ethical Relativity*. New York: Harcourt.

White, Leslie. 1939. "A Problem in Kinship Terminology." *American Anthropologist* 41:566–73.

—— 1959. *The Evolution of Culture: The Development of Civilization to the Fall of Rome*. New York: McGraw-Hill.

—— 1975. *The Concept of Cultural Systems: A Key to Understanding Tribes and Nations*. New York and London: Columbia University Press.

White, Morton. 1957. *Social Thought in America: The Revolt Against Formalism*. Boston: Beacon Press.

Whorf, Benjamin Lee. 1956. "The Relation of Habitual Thought and Behavior to Language." In *Language, Thought and Reality*. New York: Wiley.

Williams, Elgin. 1947. "Anthropology for the Common Man." *American Anthropologist* 49:84–90.

Winch, Peter. 1964. "Understanding a Primitive Society." *American Philosophical Quarterly* 1:307–24.

World Bank. 1979. *World Development Report 1979.* New York and London: Oxford University Press.

Wrong, Dennis H. 1959. "The Functional Theory of Stratification: Some Neglected Considerations." *American Sociological Review* 24:772–82.

Index